You Can't Get It Done by Doing What You Shouldn't Do

How to Stop Working So Hard at Getting What You Don't Want

DEBBIE MOREHEAD

You Can't Get It Done by Doing What You Shouldn't Do
Copyright © 2020 by Debbie Morehead

All rights reserved. This book, or parts thereof, may not be reproduced or transmitted in any form, by any means, including electronically, mechanically, photocopying, recording, or stored in an information retrieval system or otherwise, without permission from the author. Exceptions are made for brief excerpts used in published reviews.

ISBN 978-1-953586-15-5 pbk.

CONTENTS

Preface. v

Chapter 1: Why Are You Working So Hard to
           Get What You Don't Want?. 9
Chapter 2: When You Don't Get What You Want,
           This Is What Happens 25
Chapter 3: You've Got to Know Who You Are Before
           You Can Be Who You Want to Be 33
Chapter 4: You've Got to Control Yourself Before You
           Can Create Who You Want to Be (Part 1) 55
Chapter 5: You've Got to Control Yourself Before You
           Can Create Who You Want to Be (Part 2) 71
Chapter 6: You've Got to Speak Up for Yourself to
           Get More of What You Want 83
Chapter 7: You've Got to Stand Up for Yourself to
           Get More of What You Do Want 101
Chapter 8: How to Lead A Simpler Life with Better Results. . . . 107
Chapter 9: Getting More of What You Do Want 119

PREFACE

How often do you find that what you keep doing ultimately works against you?

Think about it.

How are you as a partner? Is your marriage or relationship really where you want it to be?

When it comes to your kids, how harmful was that last upsetting interaction with them?

What does your financial situation really look like? Are you spending more money than you make? Do you have tons of credit card debt? Are you always stressing about money?

What about your weight and your health?

Is your career where you truly want it to be?

The problem is that you keep working so hard but end up getting what you don't want.

There is a reason why you do everything you do—even the things that you regret and wish you hadn't done.

Most people think they are doing what they are supposed to do or should do or have the right to do in a particular situation. But then they regret their words or actions after the fact, or they get angry that something didn't go the way they wanted and blame everyone else. They work so hard to get exactly what they don't want.

As a psychotherapist of more than twenty-five years, I have seen a lot of this. More often than not, by the time people come to see me they are in tremendous pain and their life has fallen apart, but they just don't know why.

They just found out their spouse had an affair.

Their spouse just left them and is asking for a divorce.

They are constantly fighting with their spouse; they don't know how to stop it, yet they see the impact on their kids.

Their adult child isn't speaking to them, and they don't understand why.

Their teen has gotten suspended from school and is out of control.

They are constantly irritated by and yelling at their children and wondering why they behave so badly.

They've just been diagnosed with diabetes, and their doctor is telling them they must lose weight.

They are miserable and stressed in their job, but they can't afford to quit.

They are hiding from their spouse the credit card debt they have amassed, and they don't know what to do about it.

Can you relate? These types of life and relationship experiences take an emotional toll. You keep doing what you think you are supposed to be doing. You keep trying so hard and yet you keep getting the end result that you don't want. But you don't understand why, and you don't know what to do differently.

The bottom line is that you can't get it done by doing what you shouldn't be doing.

So, what should you be doing then? That is what this book will answer.

You'll learn how to stop working so hard at getting what you don't want.

There are simple, specific things you can do that will work for you, not against you.

This book will get to the bottom of why you do the things you shouldn't do—all those unhelpful actions that point you in the wrong direction in your life and relationships.

You will learn practical steps to do things differently so you can get more of what you truly want in your life and relationships.

What you *won't* get from this book is:

- a guaranteed way to always be happy
- how to indulge in your feelings
- how to prove that you are right
- how to fix your spouse or your kids
- how to change other people

If you know you need to do something different but aren't willing to do what needs to be done or if you believe you can keep doing what you are doing, thinking things will change (though they haven't for years), then this book won't help you. If you've given up on trying to change your personal relationships or you think it's everyone else's fault, then this book won't work for you.

Changing your situations and your relationships does require changing yourself. You are the way you are for a reason. You do the things you do for a reason. And yet you keep **being** and **doing** these things. You keep working so hard but not getting what you want.

If you are ready to stop working so hard getting the results you don't want, if you are willing to look at yourself and the ways you work against yourself, and if you are ready and willing to do the things you should be doing, **then keep reading.**

CHAPTER 1

Why Are You Working So Hard to Get What You Don't Want?

Life doesn't have to be as hard as you are making it.

Why are you working so hard to get what you don't want? You could be working not so hard and actually get what you really want.

I've worked with people in all areas of their lives. They have talked to me about every aspect of their life—their relationships, their marriage, their business or their job, their health, their family members, their kids, and even their friends. I've spent years listening to people tell me what they're doing. They explain in detail, "I'm doing this, and then I did that," and yet in the end, they lay out all the problems and what isn't working.

It always amazes me how hard people work to get what they don't want. Why? The truth is, you don't have to work hard to get what you actually want.

There is a better way. Stop working so hard and get the results you truly want.

I bet there are ways you are working hard but not getting what you want. Just for fun, start thinking about one thing you can stop doing that's not working for you.

Make sure to take time to pick the one thing you will stop doing so you can stop working so hard at what isn't working. Later on I'll talk about what to do that *will* work for you.

Ways People Are Working Too Hard
Money

People want more money, and they work so hard to get it. And yet they consistently go out and spend more money than they have. And then they wonder why they don't have enough money. They wonder why they don't have anything saved for retirement.

It takes more effort to outspend yourself then it does to not spend it. When you are spending more money than you have, you are constantly thinking about where you are spending it, worrying about having enough money, and anxious if you will be able to cover all your bills. It's so much more work to outspend yourself. Instead, budget and spend less than you make.

One client had built up almost seventy thousand dollars in credit card debt, all behind her husband's back. She came to me trying to figure out how to tell him. She wanted something more emotionally, and that's why she was buying stuff, but in the process, she lost her husband's trust. And she had to work much harder to rebuild that trust *and* pay off the debt.

But it doesn't even have to be that big. The number of individuals and couples I have worked with over the years that describe to me why they needed this or that and slowly build their credit card debt up and then come to me stressed or fighting over money is astounding.

Did you know that more than half of Americans spend more money than they make? Half of all Americans have some sort of credit card debt. And money is one of the top issues couples fight over?

Where are you at with your money management?

☐ Very Poor   ☐ Fairly Poor   ☐ So-So   ☐ Fairly Good   ☐ Very Good

What's one thing you can stop doing right now that isn't working for you? (stop using your credit cards, stop purchasing nonessentials, stop ignoring your bank balance, stop hiding what you are spending)

Write down one thing you will stop doing:

_____
_____
_____

Weight and Health

People work so hard to lose weight. In some ways it takes more effort to gain weight than it does to lose weight. You think about food all the time. You eat food all the time. Then you worry about your health because you are overweight or you are borderline diabetic or your cholesterol is too high.

One of my clients had been diagnosed with diabetes. He was in his sixties and about thirty pounds overweight. He was fretting a lot about it, and this caused stress and an increase in cortisol, which isn't good for the body. He was looking into all sorts of herbs and supplements and alternative treatments. Don't get me wrong; I think alternative treatments can be great, but the one thing he wasn't doing was changing his diet or increasing his exercise. Three years later his diabetes is still there and now he has to take medication, and his insulin gets out of control at times.

According to the CDC, 42 percent of Americans are obese, and 71 percent of Americans (including obesity) are overweight.

Where are you at with your health and weight management?

☐ Very Poor   ☐ Fairly Poor   ☐ So-So   ☐ Fairly Good   ☐ Very Good

What's one thing you can stop doing that isn't working for you? (stop eating late at night, stop eating while watching television, stop sitting all day long, stop going on crash diets)

Write down one thing you will stop doing:
_____
_____
_____

Significant Other Relationships

In relationships people are working harder to cause themselves more problems. If they didn't work as hard at it, they'd have better results. Instead of working harder, I teach my clients to work wiser.

The truth is that most of us have never been taught good relationship skills. We learn about relationship skills from what we see our parents do. If they didn't learn good relationship skills, then you aren't going to learn them either. And we certainly didn't learn these skills in school.

We are stuck doing what we observed growing up. When I begin working with a new client or couple, I ask questions about their experiences growing up. I ask how their parents or primary caregivers showed affection, and I ask them to describe their parent's relationship as well.

It never fails that in some ways, often without even realizing it, they have repeated some of the same behaviors and ways of interacting in their relationship.

Typically the stuff we hated that our parents did when we were growing up gets played out in our relationship with our partner.

One man that came to see me as he was going through his third divorce. After helping him with the immediate issues of moving out and figuring out how to co-parent, we then delved into all those questions about his growing up and his past. I wanted to make sure he saw how hard he was working at repeating the same pattern, three marriages later! I wanted to help him to stop all that hard work and go on to create what he really wanted in a significant other relationship. We made connections between the patterns in his marriages to patterns in his youth that were being repeated. He told me he went home after that summary session and sat in shock for several hours that evening. As we were ending therapy, he said to me, "I wish I had come to you a lot sooner; it would have saved me so much hard work and pain."

Most of us have heard the divorce rate is around 50 percent, but did you know that the chances of divorce increase (not decrease!) with second and third marriages? The divorce rate is 67 percent and 73 percent respectively. It's not that we get smarter and learn to do it better—we just repeat it all again. Working harder once again!

There are reasons why we fight the way we fight, why we protect ourselves the way we do when we get hurt in our relationships, and why we react to our significant other's behavior the way we do. It's time to stop doing things that make it harder on you and your relationship and start doing what works.

> Where are you at with your significant other relationship?
>
> ☐ Very Poor   ☐ Fairly Poor   ☐ So-So   ☐ Fairly Good   ☐ Very Good
>
> What's one thing you can stop doing that isn't working for you?
>
> (Stop holding grudges, criticizing, defining you partner in absolutes, using words like *always* and *never*, giving your partner the silent treatment, fighting)
>
> Write down one thing you will stop doing:
>
> _____
> _____
> _____

Raising Children

Children are the lights of our life, so they say. And yet you'd never know it when they do something they aren't supposed to that make us mad. How quickly mean words or even actions fly out of us in those moments!

For years I worked with children in the foster care system who had been taken away from their parents because of some sort of abuse. Hopefully you have not had your children taken away, but when you think about how you handled that last upsetting interaction with your child, how did it go? Did you respond or did you react? Did you let yourself get out of control and say hurtful words that actually caused emotional damage to your child?

Studies conducted over the years clearly connect parental discipline with a child's moral development. John and Julie Gottman's research show that the two predictors of how a child turns out is 1) the skill and ability to understand and manage their feelings and 2) how they get along with adults and other children. How you parent and how you discipline play a major factor in the development of these areas for your child.

So, how do you want your child to grow and develop?

I have spent a large percentage of my career teaching foster parents, adoptive parents, biological parents, and group home staff how to manage themselves when they are upset so they can actually parent in a way that truly helps their child to learn and grow from their own mistakes. Isn't that what we all want? Yet it's not what we do. We get emotional and work hard to make sure our kids know what *they did wrong*. And then we wonder why our kids behave so badly or turn out the way they do.

One couple came to me knowing that the way they were dealing with their son and daughter was not helpful (thank goodness for that) but not knowing what to do. At first each spouse just wanted me to tell the other spouse what they were doing wrong, because, as is the norm, they had very different ways of parenting. One was way too lenient, and the other was way too stern. As a result they were doing a lot of fighting among themselves. I started by helping them talk about why they had children in the first place and what they both truly desired for their children. Once there was a shared purpose, we then looked at how each of them had been parented growing up and how they were playing some of that out in the present. He was way too lenient because he never wanted his kids to feel how he felt with his abusive dad. She was too stern partly because he was too lenient and she felt she needed to "pick up the slack." She also thought that, although she was stern, she wasn't anything like her mother who was controlling and had overly high expectations, which resulted in verbal abuse when not met. Next we defined what they wanted the environment in their household to look like. I taught them how to manage their emotions when they were upset, and I reminded them that punishment in the upset moment is never helpful. Next we created some rules and structure. Finally I taught them a variety of ways to discipline so their children would actually learn from each incident, and I taught them other ways to be more emotionally available for their kids. The one thing that both parents wanted more than anything was to have a peaceful home. And that is exactly what they created.

> Where do you stand when it comes to parenting without damaging your children?
>
> ☐ Very Poor   ☐ Fairly Poor   ☐ So-So   ☐ Fairly Good   ☐ Very Good
>
> What's one thing you can stop doing that isn't working for you?
> (stop fighting with your partner over the kids, stop yelling at your kids, stop hitting your kids, stop parenting the way you were parented, stop trying to control your kids.)
>
> Write down one thing you will stop doing:
> _____
> _____
> _____

Family Relationships

So let's be real, we love our parents, but there are things we hate about them. The truth is that for better or worse, our parents are our parents, with all their strengths and weaknesses.

When I work with a new client, I always ask them to share three strengths and three weaknesses of each of their primary caregivers as well as a few memories with each parent. This gives me a clearer picture of the relationship with their parents and the physical, mental, and emotional experience they had growing up.

In an ideal world, once we become an adult, our parents are able to continue to be support persons while allowing us to move into our own life. In a not-so-ideal world, they either become over-involved and try to control us or they are so busy with their own life that they aren't really available for us. In most cases this is how we experienced them as we were growing up.

A client asked me to help her with a big frustration she felt toward her mom that had been consuming her for quite a while. For the past two years, her mom had a boyfriend, and there were two issues that bothered her. One was that her mother spent almost no time with her grandchildren, and the other was that during one of the family gatherings, the boyfriend had gotten drunk and said some mean things to my client's husband. She and I spent time connecting that her being consumed with this situation was tied to similar experiences she had growing up with her alcoholic father. Her mom had never defended her and focused more on her dad than on her and her siblings. Once she understood this, it reduced her anger, and she stopped obsessing about it and trying to change her mother. Together we came up with an effective way to communicate positive requests to her mother. In the end, though the boyfriend stayed, my client and her mom improved their relationship, and her mom started spending more time with the grandchildren.

Family relationships are almost always a point of discussion when I work with a client. Our parents and family members are part of our life, and when things don't go well, we work hard at trying to fix them. Often we try to get the other person to be different and then are constantly disappointed that they don't meet our expectations.

> Where do you stand in your relationship with your parents and family members?
>
> ☐ Very Poor ☐ Fairly Poor ☐ So-So ☐ Fairly Good ☐ Very Good
>
> What's one thing you can stop doing that isn't working for you?
> (stop trying to get your parent to be different, stop playing the same role you did growing up (i.e., trying to fix everything), stop holding a grudge)
>
> Write down one thing you will stop doing:
>
> _____
> _____
> _____

Friendships

We all need connections and support people in our lives. But sometimes even those relationships let us down. We keep trying to do something to make the relationship better, or we just terminate the relationship but then continue to hold anger and hurt toward that person, which is exhausting.

I spoke with a woman who shared a painful interaction she had in college with her best friend at the time. When we spoke, the relationship had ended about three years prior, but she was still thinking about it, still feeling confused and hurt. She and I went over the incidents that had led up to the demise of the friendship. We connected that there was a consistent way of interacting with her friend that reminded her of a painful way of interacting with her mom. Then we spent some time looking at the situation from her friend's point of view. This allowed her to let go of the hurt she was holding on to. Two years later she called me to let me know that she had reconnected up with that friend at a reunion, talked about what had happened during a helpful discussion, and was able to rekindle the friendship again.

Where are your friendships like?

☐ Very Poor   ☐ Fairly Poor   ☐ So-So   ☐ Fairly Good   ☐ Very Good

What's one thing you can stop doing that isn't working for you?
(stop holding grudges, stop trying to be the one to always fix things, stop tolerating a behavior that you don't like)

Write down one thing you will stop doing:

_____
_____
_____

Jobs

According to a 2018 Gallup poll, 66 percent of people are not engaged or even actively disengaged in their jobs. If you are in this category, it may not mean you hate your job, but you're not exactly happy with your job either. And yet we spend about one-third (ninety thousand hours) of our life in a job.

We go to work because we have to make a living, but does that mean we have to be dissatisfied eight hours a day? There are many reasons people are disengaged with their job. It may be with the actual job itself, it may be dealing with your boss or co-workers, it may be the pay, or it may be that there is no room for growth or no recognition for what you do.

I know you need to keep a job in order to support yourself and your family, but do you need to keep working so hard at something you're not really enjoying?

I worked with a nurse who actually did enjoy her actual job, but she dreaded going to work because of one of her co-workers. The co-worker was quite controlling and critical of the other nurses in the clinic. After spending some time talking about specific interactions, she shared what she knew about this co-worker. She mentioned that the co-worker had been a charge nurse in a previous job, but that clinic had closed down. With that new information and a few prepared statements such as "Wow, you know your stuff!" or "That's a good way to think about it," we came up with a plan for how she could win over her co-worker. And she did! Now she really enjoys going to work every day.

How would you rate your job satisfaction?

☐ Very Poor   ☐ Fairly Poor   ☐ So-So   ☐ Fairly Good   ☐ Very Good

What's one thing you can stop doing that isn't working for you?
(stop focusing on what you hate about your job, stop complaining about your boss, stop finding ways to do your job half-heartedly)

Write down one thing you will stop doing:

_____

_____

_____

Business

People say they want to get more clients so they can build their business, but what do they do? They spend money to hire a branding coach or they hire a copywriter to work on their website or they work on creating their program. But they forget to just ask people to do business with them.

It's easy when building a business to get busy doing things that won't actual build your business and won't get the clients you need to sustain your business. That's why approximately 20 percent of businesses fail in the first year, and 50 percent fail within the fifth year.

If you own a business, where are you at with your business success?

☐ Very Poor   ☐ Fairly Poor   ☐ So-So   ☐ Fairly Good   ☐ Very Good

What's one thing you can stop doing that isn't working for you?
(stop spending money on your website, stop hiding behind your computer, stop taking every class or program always looking for the next new idea)

Write down one thing you will stop doing:

_____
_____
_____

Now that you have some examples of how others are working too hard but still not getting what they want and you've thought about small first steps of what you can stop doing to get closer to the results you want, let's look at the reasons why people tend to stay where they are at, being unhappy, working too hard, and not getting what they want.

Why People Stay Stuck

Here are some reasons I've found in working with my clients that, in spite of not getting the results they want, they still keep doing what they're doing.

Reason #1: You are sure you are doing what you're supposed to be doing.

You think you know what to do, but it actually is not the right thing. You think you know, but you don't. In reality you're in an unaware place, and this will cost you over time.

Usually these people don't come in for therapy; however, I often see them when their spouse threatens them with divorce unless they see a therapist or the courts get involved regarding their kids or a DUI.

Reason #2: You admit that you don't know what you need to know, but you don't know what will really work.

You lack the correct information. You know that you don't have a clue what you are supposed to be doing. In other words, you know that you don't know what you don't know. But until you gather the right information, things will stay the same.

Hopefully that's why you are reading this book.

Reason #3: It's not a priority.

You actually know what you should be doing, but you just don't want to do it. It's not a priority for you since you don't think things are that bad (yet!), or you are hurt and angry and not willing to do anything different—you don't believe it will really work anyway.

Reason #4: You're trying but not executing effectively.

You know what to do, but you are executing it the wrong way. Things only work if you do them the *right way*. It takes practice to learn something new and make it a habit.

Reason #5: You've given up.

You settle and tolerate. You are doing things the only way you know how and playing out old patterns, and you believe that's just the way it is.

Are any of these familiar to you?

So What's Next?

By this time you should be asking yourself, "Why am I doing all that when I'm still not getting the results I want?"

I've never met anybody that wasn't doing this in some area of their life. I do it too. There are times in my life when I have to step back and look at my results and ask myself, "Why am I exhausted from doing this and yet I still don't have the results I want? What have I done wrong?"

When people are heading in the wrong direction, they tend to go further down the rabbit hole before they realize that this rabbit hole still won't get them what they actually want.

In the next chapter we will look at where most people tend to go when they finally realize they aren't getting what they want. See if this sounds like you. I bet it does.

CHAPTER 2

When You Don't Get What You Want, This Happens

When you finally step back, look at your results, and question why you are doing what you do but not getting what you want, then what do you do?

We all do one of two things, and often we go back and forth between the two.

What are those two things? We either blame ourselves, or we blame another person.

> Shame, blame, disrespect, betrayal, and the withholding of affection damage the roots from which love grows. Love can only survive these injuries if they are acknowledged, healed and rare.
> —Brene Brown

Just think about the last time you didn't get what you wanted or someone didn't meet your expectations. What did you do? What went through your mind? All sorts of negative thoughts about yourself OR all sorts of negative thoughts about the other person, right? Be honest with yourself.

Let's be real.

When You Blame Yourself, It Looks Like This

Unhappy in his marriage, one of my clients said, "I was hanging out with my golf buddies, and we were talking about marriage. One had been sleeping on his couch for over a year, one was having an affair, and the other hadn't had sex with his wife for over five years. All along I was thinking that they were the schmucks living in unhappy marriages. And then it hit me: I'm one of them too."

A young man who was turning twenty-one sat in my office, depressed, telling me what a failure he was. He couldn't seem to get anything right, unlike his father, who at age twenty-three had purchased his own house. He explained he had moved out with a partner and tried to make it on his own, but the relationship ended badly and he had to move back home because he was unable to afford the apartment. "I tried so hard," he said sadly, "but I just can't get anything right."

A woman's husband had an affair, and all she could think about was "What's wrong with me? Is it because I gained weight? Is it because I was at work too much? There must be something wrong with me."

She'd been going to Weight Watchers and trying to lose weight for over a year. She'd lose and then gain over and over again. She came to me after receiving a new diagnosis of pre-diabetes. At that point she believed there was just something wrong with her because she could never succeed at anything.

On top of that, the school called because her twelve-year-old daughter had gotten into a fight. She was expelled for a week, and the school wanted to talk about possibly moving her to a continuation school because of her attitude and bad grades. At the end of the meeting, all this woman could think was "I'm such a horrible parent—what am I doing wrong?"

Her inner dialogue continued.

"Yes, I wanted him to back me up when our daughter left a mess in the kitchen. But I got so angry when he said to let her finish watching her show first. I said such mean things. What is wrong with me? I'm so stupid."

"My dad left me and moved to another state when I was thirteen, and now twenty years later, my husband is leaving me. What is so wrong with me that no man wants to stay?"

"My credit cards are maxed out, and I'm barely living paycheck to paycheck. Why can't I figure out how to manage my money? I'm such an idiot."

This is where we all find ourselves at times. "I'm an idiot!" "What's wrong with me?" "I'll never get it right." "Nothing ever works out for me." And we head down the path of feeling bad about ourselves. Feeling bad that we have let ourselves and our family down. We start putting ourselves down; we feel depressed about our lives. We go down the rabbit hole of self-defeat.

"Maybe it was the color of my lipstick or the dress I wore. I'm so ugly, that's why he didn't ask me on a second date."

"Maybe it's my voice. Maybe it's the way I dress. Maybe I'm just not smart enough. No one will ever hire me. What's wrong with me?"

"I'm such a loser. If only I looked like Matthew McConaughey, maybe she wouldn't have left me."

"If only I was the perfect, patient parent, my kids would never get in trouble. I'll never get it right!"

And on and on.

> "Nothing ever goes how I want it to go. What's wrong with me? It's all my fault! I'm such an idiot!"

But . . .

Most people don't like to stay in that place for long. It's a little too painful to sit and believe it's all our fault. That's when we take the focus off of ourselves and blame others instead.

> When you blame others, you give up your power to change.
> —Robert Anthony

When You Blame Others, It Looks Like This

He reluctantly came to my office with his wife only after she threatened to leave him after three weeks of him not talking to her. He looked at me and gladly recounted what a horrible thing she did to have hugged her ex at her daughter's wedding and that's why the silence, stating clearly, "I'm only here to make sure you know that I'm right and this is all her fault."

"My boss is such an idiot. How could she have given me a low score on my evaluation? I've been working here eleven years. I know what I'm doing, and I do an excellent job. She's only been here two years, and she knows nothing about my job. She's just trying to impress her boss. She's such a jerk."

"If you had just helped me out with the kids, then we wouldn't have gotten in the argument and we would have had sex. So it's your fault we aren't going to have sex."

"My kids should listen when I tell them what to do. I shouldn't have to tell my son to stop picking on his little sister that many times or to repeatedly tell him to pick up his toys. If he'd just listen better, I wouldn't get so mad. He's so bad."

She explained to her husband that if only he had paid more attention to her instead of working all the time, she wouldn't have spent so much money and built up all that credit card debt. She absolutely stood her ground that it was his fault that she spent so much money.

I could share many more examples of blaming others. In addition to believing it's all someone else's fault, people then think it's a good idea to tell them just how wrong they are.

Of course, this only makes things worse. We've all experienced this. We are so convinced that we are right and they are wrong. We get into verbal fighting matches about who is wrong, or we silence out people for weeks. Nothing gets resolved. We dig our heels in deeper, and in the process, we do more damage as we work harder only to get the opposite of what we want. We create disconnect, burn bridges, and in some cases do permanent damage.

"It's not my fault—it's your fault!"

"It's not my fault—it's *their* fault!"

All you know is that it's not *your* fault.

"I was so close to winning. The slot machines are set up to trick you; that's why I kept playing and lost my money. It's the casino's fault!"

"My business failed because my competition lied. It's their fault!"

"If you hadn't been talking, I wouldn't have backed into the mailbox. It's your fault!"

"I wouldn't be overweight if they hadn't put corn syrup in everything. It's their fault!"

"I wouldn't have thrown the computer if it didn't keep freezing on me. It's the computer's fault!"

Get the point?

> Think for a minute about the last few upsets that occurred in your life or relationships.
>
> What are a few of the things you said to yourself when you were in the "It's all my fault" place?
>
> _____
> _____
> _____
>
> What were the last blaming statements you said inside your head or even told someone?
>
> _____
> _____
> _____
>
> How did all that work out for you? Did it get you closer to what you wanted?

> Which rabbit hole do you choose?
> Blaming yourself or blaming others: Does either option really work?

Now What?

Now you have an abundantly clear picture that you are working way too hard and still not getting what you want. And you've gone down one or both of the rabbit holes—either it's all your fault or it's all their fault. What can you do about it?

That's why you are reading this book. In the next chapters I am going to explain exactly what you can do to stop working so hard, not getting the results you want. And I'll show you what you can do to get the results you want in your life and relationships.

Since we tend to be our own worst enemies in all this, it all starts with making sure you really know yourself first. And that is where we are going next.

CHAPTER 3

You've Got to Know Who You Are Before You Can Be Who You Want to Be

> To know thyself is the beginning of wisdom.
> —Socrates

"Why did I say that?" "Why did I do that?" Have you ever found yourself asking these questions? Most of us have.

If you really want to stop working so hard at not getting what you want, then it all begins by understanding why you are the way you are. You need to understand who you are and why you are that way. You can't change what you don't understand.

What I'm really talking about here is self-awareness. Let's talk about what that really means. Why are you the way you are?

To really know yourself means that you understand:

- Why you do the things you do
- Why you think the way you think
- Why you react the way you react

What You're Taught

The bottom line is that it all starts with what happened while you were growing up. What went on around you while you were growing up is the way you learned about everything.

Most everything comes from your past. What you experienced, what was modeled for you, how you were treated, what you observed, and the conclusions your child brain made all have resulted in why you are the way you are today.

Why do you cook the roast that way? Probably because you watched your mom cook the roast that way. So you say, "That's just how it's done."

You do what you do and the way you do it because there was an example set for you or you were trained to do it that way or your observations led you to believe that was what worked for you.

It works in the way you think about things—from politics and religion to male/female roles and business, from how you handle your money to how you handle your relationships. The way you handle your money is probably the way your parents handled money. Your work ethic comes from the way you watched your parents work. The way you handle conflict is probably how your parents handled conflict with each other and with you.

So you've got to know who you are and why you are that way. You've got to know why you act the way you do, why you think the way you think, and why you react the way you react. If you want to stop working so hard, not getting the results you want, you need to know yourself.

> If you want to stop working so hard, not getting the results you want, you need to know yourself.

I was working with a man who had cheated on his wife. As we dug deeper, he constantly talked about feeling guilty about talking to his wife about problems or the things that stressed him, so it was easier, in the moment to be with this other woman who didn't ask questions and had no expectations of him. Not surprisingly, he had a father with a bad temper, and he watched his mother do everything to try to avoid making his dad mad. As a child he learned to escape into his room to avoid making his dad mad. So avoiding conflict was the only way he knew how to handle things, and that's what he did when he cheated on his wife. As a result, he had to work a lot harder to regain her trust.

I worked with another couple who illustrates this. She had a very high-strung, emotionally explosive mother that was often verbally abusive, so as a child she learned to people-please to avoid the explosions. He had a dad that managed his anger poorly and at times was out of control in his physical punishment of the kids, so he learned that's what you do when you are angry. They found each other, fell in love, and got married. Off they went into a crazy pattern of her avoiding him when he got mad, which only made him madder. They finally came to see me after a verbal fighting match in a mall parking lot with a crowd staring at them finally made them realize something was definitely not working. They were working way too hard to gain each other's understanding. They never resolved anything and instead were damaging their relationship.

It never fails—the way we are and the things we do in our adult life and relationships are directly tied to experiences we had growing up.

After gathering information from my clients about their background at the beginning of our sessions together, I then share my assessment. I always share with them a piece that I call "it's not surprising that . . ."

It's not surprising that . . .

- you chose a husband that was emotionally abusive when your stepmom was as emotionally abusive as she was,
- you are overweight and have a difficult time taking care of yourself because your mom's depression taught you that taking care of her was more important than taking care of yourself,
- you take the easy way out when it comes to work and have lost jobs because you watched your dad take the easy way out in jobs and never finish jobs,
- you don't know how to manage your emotions and explode because that was how your parents dealt with their feelings.
- you are extremely hard on yourself and have a loud critical voice because your mother was often very critical of you.

I'm going to dive a little deeper, but stick with me. In order to stop doing what you shouldn't do you need to know and understand yourself better and this is how you do it.

Why You Do the Things You Do

If we know that more than half of Americans spend more money than they make, 71 percent of Americans are overweight, 45 percent of marriages end in divorce, between 15 and 43 percent of marriages experience infidelity (everyone lies about this one), and half of businesses fail within the fifth year of business, then we know that too many people are working way too hard but getting the opposite of what they want.

Why do we do things that get us the exact opposite results of what we want?

More often than not if you asked someone "Why did you have an affair?" "Why did you let yourself gain so much weight?" or "Why did you spend so much money?" they would come up with all sorts of explanations. But they wouldn't come up with the real reason.

- "If she had just had sex with me, I wouldn't have cheated on her."
- "I was planning to start a diet tomorrow."
- "I really wanted that new car; I deserve it."

The real why is always more difficult to get to and understand.

Getting to the real why is about your deeper needs. About your emotional needs. Part of knowing yourself is actually knowing what it is you really need so you can make sure you get those needs met instead of doing things that in the moment feel good but in the long run work against you and what you really want.

A sixteen-year-old foster girl was placed in a group home after being kicked out of several foster homes. She was one of seven siblings, all who were in foster care and spread out into several different foster homes and group homes. She had been in foster care since she was six years old. Shortly after being placed in the group home, there was a major upset, and in her anger, she broke five windows. She had some consequences, such as extra chores, to make up for the cost. The group home supervisor and I were tasked to find out more about what was going on with her and what she really needed. Obviously breaking windows definitely would keep getting her the opposite of what she wanted. It was clear that with her history, she needed to know she was significant, that she mattered in this world, since that had not been her experience so far.

We set out to make sure she knew that she mattered. The group home supervisor started spending more time with her. We located some of her siblings and set up visits to reconnect her with them. I discovered that because she had moved so much throughout her life and missed so many important school lessons, she only read at a second-grade level. We brought in an educational therapist who in a short time got her reading level beyond the sixth grade. We gave her the attention she needed and deserved. This helped her to begin to feel like she mattered, and she slowly began to feel better about herself.

The next time there was a major blow out at the group home, instead of breaking windows she wrote all her upset thoughts on the back of her bedroom door with a permanent marker. That was an easy fix by comparison! She and her supervisor painted over the door, and to those of us working with her, this was GREAT PROGRESS! Things only got better from there. She successfully left the group home, reconnected with her family, graduated from high school, and got a decent job. All because we took time to find out and meet what she really needed.

I know this is a more extreme example, but in some way this is what we all do. This is why we do the things we do that work against us. We have underlying needs that often we aren't even aware of, and we act out in ways that will never work for us. Working with kids in the foster care system, it was my job to figure out what those unmet needs were for each child. When my colleagues and I found ways to start meeting those needs, things turned around for each child. And the same can be true for you.

Remember, when we are little kids, we all have deeper emotional needs, but it's not like we know what they are. We don't feel that we could ever walk up to our mom or dad and say, "I need more attention" or "I need to feel safe."

In addition to not even knowing what our own needs are, somewhere along the way, we figure out that having needs is a weakness or that it isn't OK to ask for what we really want or need. It makes us too vulnerable because what if we ask and they don't meet our need? Then we'll really know we're not important or lovable or . . .

The problem is that when things are below the surface, at an unconscious level, they come out whether you like it or not, and in the end they get in your way. This is why you end up asking yourself, "Why did I do that?" time and time again.

Patricia Miles, a consultant I often worked with, always reminded us that bad behavior is a result of an unmet need. And the same is true for you and me.

> Bad behavior is a result of an unmet need.
> —Patricia Miles

Just like working with those foster kids, identify their needs, and intentionally helping to meet them helped them to make better choices for themselves, the same is true for you. When you identify your needs, you will be able to make better choices. You will be able to catch your negative behaviors before you act on them. You'll better understand why you're feeling and thinking the way you are and make better choices that work for you and toward what you want.

When talking about unmet needs, it is not the things we often think of like "I need money" or "I need a car." Remember, you do what you do and the way you do it because of what you experienced growing up and the conclusions you drew from those experiences.

In most cases our parents do the best they can. But not all of our needs, especially our emotional needs, are fully met. That's why we all can behave so badly and regret our behaviors after the fact.

Based on various circumstances in which you felt or experienced certain emotional needs not being fully met, you created beliefs about yourself. Whether you know it or not, you behave according to these beliefs, which is what often makes you work hard trying to get those needs met but instead getting the opposite results.

- She was the fourth of five siblings, and both her parents had to work a lot of hours to support the family. She believed she wasn't that significant because of often not being included.
- Her dad was an alcoholic, and her mom and dad fought a lot. She felt unloved and thought that she wasn't worthy of attention.
- He grew up in a poor and dangerous neighborhood and experienced watching his dad hitting his mom. He felt unsafe and like he had no control.

Why you are the way you are and do the things you do, often behaving badly, working hard but not getting what you want, all starts with your unmet childhood needs.

Chloe Madanes in her work on Human Needs psychology have identified four core emotional needs: love/connection, significance, certainty, and variety. For your first step, identify your top two unmet emotional needs.

Let's Identify Your Need(s):

Love/Connection	Significance	Certainty	Variety
belonging	important	safety/safe	independence
acceptance	worthy	security	joy
loved	good enough	consistency	spontaneity
cared for	attention	stable	freedom
desired/adored	valued	in control	choices
included	be seen	peaceful/peace	adventure
approved of	be noticed	protected	unrestricted
affection	be heard	predictable	self-reliant
understood	appreciated	informed	excitement
known	recognized	being OK	change

> Choose your top two out of these four. Which two did you most feel you didn't get enough of growing up or would have liked more of?
>
> Category: _____ Word: _____
>
> Create a personalized sentence: _____
>
> Category: _____ Word: _____
>
> Create a personalized sentence: _____
>
> Examples:
>
> Category: Significance   Word: Important
>
> Create a personalized sentence: I need to feel important.
>
> Category: Certainty   Word: Consistency
>
> Create a personalized sentence: I need to experience consistency.
>
> Category: Love/Connection   Word: Loved
>
> Create a personalized sentence: I need to feel loved.
>
> Category: Variety   Word: Choices
>
> Create a personalized sentence: I need to know I have choices.
>
> If you have a different word than you see on my list that fits under one of those four categories, choose that one since it's your need.

Now that you know that your underlying emotional needs often come out in your behaviors, get in your way, and end up making you work way too hard getting bad results, let's look at how those needs shape the way you think and end up working against you.

Why You Think the Way You Think

You think the way you think because it's what you were told growing up. It's what you watched your parents do, and then you came to the conclusion that this is how you should think about yourself, about others, and about the world.

The conclusions you come to, how you think about yourself, others, and the world around you grow out of your unmet needs.

These then become a belief (what you think) that seeps into how you behave. More often than not, you aren't even aware of these beliefs, but they constantly impact the choices you make every day of your life.

These beliefs then limit how you think, what you do or don't do, and how you behave in certain situations.

This is how it looks. As children we believe everything is about us or is our fault (it's an egocentric position). So if our mother is depressed and crying a lot, we automatically think it is something about us or that we did something to make her cry. If our parents don't do a good job of letting us know that upsetting situations aren't about us, we come to negative conclusions about ourselves. Or if our parent was upset with something we did but handled it with unkind or demeaning words, we assume what our parents say about us is the truth. During stressful or difficult situations, we begin to define ourselves, others, and even the world.

- Her mother was very perfectionistic and controlling, and even after she finished her homework or cleaned the bathroom, her mother would come back and redo it or tell her she did it wrong and make her do it again. She concluded, "I'm not good enough."
- His dad didn't know how to control his anger, and when he'd get upset, he would call him names and hit him. He concluded, "I'm unlovable and others aren't safe."

- She was born to a seventeen-year-old mother and was the oldest of five siblings, one who had special needs. She concluded, "I'm not worthy of attention."
- Her mother had anxiety, always believed the worst-case scenario, and was controlling and overly protective. Her mother didn't let her do most normal childhood things. She concluded, "I have no choices in my life."
- He grew up in a gang-infested area and observed domestic violence between his mom and stepdad. He concluded, "The world is unsafe, and I'm invisible."

The conclusions we tell ourselves as children become beliefs we hold that then come out in how we think and live. These beliefs limit us in how we are in our life and in our relationships. Limiting beliefs become connected to the way we define ourselves, others, and the world around us. They come out in our actions, interactions, and choices.

> Limiting beliefs become connected to the way we define ourselves, others, and the world around us.
> They come out in our actions, interactions, and choices.

Let's take your identified unmet needs from the previous exercise and turn them into your limiting beliefs. You need to know what these are since you have been operating from these places that have been working against you.

> **Let's Identify Your Limiting Beliefs:**
>
> Take your needs statements from above and turn them into "I believe" statements:
>
> I believe I'm _____.
>
> or I believe others are _____.
>
> For example: "I believe I'm unimportant."
> "I believe others are never consistent."
> "I believe I'm unlovable."
> "I believe I have no choices in life."
>
> Belief #1 _____
>
> Belief #2 _____

I'm not going to leave you stuck here. The whole point of this book is to get you more of what you want in your life and relationships. But it starts with knowing why you are the way you are. Later on I will walk you through switching these limiting beliefs to empowering beliefs so that you can move forward. As I say to my clients at this point, "Don't worry, I'm not going to leave you here. Understanding and knowing yourself is the start. The whole purpose of knowing yourself is to be able to change yourself. And I will help you do this."

Back to next steps of knowing yourself.

Now that you know your unmet emotional needs and how those have become limiting beliefs that get in the way in your life, let's look at the ways they come out and really work against you. Let's examine how they keep you from getting what you want and often creating exactly the opposite of what you want.

Why You React the Way You React

You react the way you do because of what you experienced growing up. When you experience certain things over and over again growing up, these become your hot spots, your trigger points. Your hot spots (triggers) come from the experiences you have growing up and the meaning you put on those experiences, and when something in your present day creates a similar feeling, you react to it.

As a child, when you experienced those situations over and over again, you came up with ways to handle your feelings. You came up with ways to protect or defend yourself from those difficult situations, feelings, and experiences.

Let's start with knowing what sets you off.

Hot Spots (Triggers)

If you at least know your hot spots (triggers), you won't be surprised when something happens and you fly off the handle.

Of course, in the moment, you might still step back after your reaction and say, "That even surprised me."

Every one of us have experienced this. Somebody said something to you or did something, and it hit you wrong.

Your hot spots come from all the different difficult or stressful experiences you've had growing up—experiences with your parents, with your siblings, at school with your friends and teachers.

It's what gets you riled up.

There is an exercise I take couples through after they have had a bad fight. It helps to connect their past experiences growing up to their present reaction. I have adapted it from work of John Gottman and Gary Brainerd, and it goes like this:

I have them describe the facts of the situation what each person said and did.

> I was vacuuming, and I accidentally vacuumed up a small Lego. My son saw it and got upset and started crying. I told him I was sorry and that when I was done vacuuming, we could go through the vacuum bag contents and find it. My son then told his dad, and his dad came and got the vacuum cleaner and took it outside and found the Lego. When he came back in, I yelled at my husband, and then I didn't talk to him for three days.

Then they describe their perception of the situation, which includes their thoughts and meanings they put on the situation.

> It seemed he cared more about our son than me. He didn't even ask me what happened. He didn't work with me on this issue.

Next I have them describe their feelings and have them connect those feelings to any underlying fear around them.

> I felt discounted, disrespected. My underlying fear is that I'm not seen, like my side doesn't matter.

The next step, and it's an important one, is for them to connect to past moments or experiences where they had similar feelings from childhood memories and then share that experience with their partner and connect to that childhood wound. The goal is to get them connected to that deeper desire around their unmet need.

> This reminds me of all the times growing up with my little sister. She had some special needs. Whenever we'd be playing and she got upset, she'd hit me. Sometimes she'd hit me for no reason

at all, but every time I'd hit her back, I'd be the one that got in trouble. I never got to explain my side of things. So when my spouse came and got the vacuum without talking to me, it reminded me of those feelings as a kid that my side didn't matter.

Only then do I move into helping them to take responsibility for their reactive/protective behavior, apologize, and come up with what they can do differently next time.

I'm sorry for yelling at you and then cutting you off and not talking to you for three days. That wasn't fair of me. Next time I will ask you to stop what you are doing and talk to me first.

I also encourage them to think of and ask for what their partner could do differently next time as well.

What could have helped me would have been for you to come ask me first about what happened with the Lego instead of just siding with our son.

Our hot spots (triggers) more often than not are connected to big feelings about something from our past experiences.
Believe it or not, the majority of times when you overreact, it is tied to feelings and experiences from your past. It is tied to your past thoughts and feelings around those unmet needs from childhood. These are often tied to your parents or primary caregivers' weaknesses or negative character traits.
If you react because a car is barreling toward you, that is normal human instinct. But if you react (overreact) because your child throws

something, your boss yells at your, or your spouse didn't help bring in the groceries, that overreaction is coming from your past stuff.

We will get into what to do about your triggers in the next chapter, but for now let's identify your triggers.

Let's Identify Your Hot Spots (Triggers):

List three to four weaknesses of each of your primary caregivers (critical, controlling, impatient, not there, overprotective, angry, anxious, depressed, sarcastic)

mom _____

dad _____

other _____

Here is a list of additional triggers: (put a checkmark by your triggers)

_____ distant _____ cold _____ preoccupied

_____ hard to please _____ controlling

_____ disapproving _____ critical _____ never there

_____ neglected _____ anxious _____ overprotective

_____ impatient _____ depressed angry _____ sarcastic

_____ stubborn _____ being used _____ rejection

_____ selfish/self-absorbed _____ no filter

_____ not affectionate/undemonstrative _____ smothered

_____ feeling invisible

____ other (_____) ____ other (_____)

____ other (_____) ____ other (_____)

And that leads us to how you react, the actions you take in these situations. The ways you handle these difficult situations stem from what you learned in your childhood, and you are still doing them in your adult relationships. Once again, you are working too hard in the wrong direction and not getting what you want. Let's talk about the ways you handle things when you are triggered.

How You Handle It (Protectors)

The way you handle difficult or painful situations growing up comes from either what you've seen modeled by your parents and how they handled stress and difficulties or the conclusions you've come to in your child brain that seems to work in that situation at the time. The problem is that you now take this way of trying to protect yourself from the stress or pain into handling similar situations in your adult life and relationships. In most cases what you created during your childhood to protect yourself very seldom works successfully in your adult relationships and adult situations.

It becomes your fallback position of handling things, but it pretty much works against you. For example:

- Your fallback position is to go to the refrigerator when you are depressed or upset.
- Your fallback position is to seek comfort from spending money, so you go online and buy something.
- Your fallback position is to go hide and bury your head under the covers and play the "woe is me" game when you feel sad or hurt.
- Your fallback position is to scream at everybody in your family when you are angry.

Experiences in your past told you that is the way to handle it.
What's your fallback position? You've got at least one. We all do.

Everybody has a place they go to when something happens, with their kids, their spouse, their business, their customers, their money, their health. You've got a place you go to.

It's your toolbox, the way you handle things, the way you protect yourself from painful, difficult situations.

But remember, those tools were created from a child's understanding. So they don't work very well in adult situations. More often than not, they work against you and make things harder on you.

- Her parents were overprotective and controlling and didn't let her do any of the normal kid stuff. She learned to rebel and crawl out of the window to do what she wanted. In her adult life, her boss is overbearing and controlling. She says yes to his face, but behind his back she does what she wants to do which has led to three write-ups.
- When there was conflict in his family, everyone yelled but made up easily afterward. In his business and marriage, that's what he does too. He continually has to hire new people because his employees keep quitting, and his wife is demanding he go to therapy or else.
- She watched her mom people-please when her dad was upset. In her marriage she runs around trying to people-please and make everything OK with her husband, but inside she is resentful.
- She learned that saying whatever was on your mind and exploding is how to communicate because that is how her great aunt (her primary caregiver) communicated. In her adult life she says what is on her mind at work and in her relationships, but this has led to her getting fired, and she is heading toward her second divorce.

- When there was tension and conflict, he watched his dad disappear and go to the garage. With his kids and wife, he avoids conflict and disappears into his man cave, where he plays video games for hours. His kids and wife feel sad and disconnected.

We ALL do this; we just have our own version. What we saw as kids and how we figured out how to handle stressful, difficult situations is what we continue to repeat in all areas of our life.

These are our protectors, our fallback positions. It's the old, skimpy toolbox we use to ward off unpleasant feelings that arise in stressful or difficult situations. They are automatic, but for the most part they work against us. The way we protect ourselves in psychological terms is called "default defense mechanisms." As Freud says, they "are psychological strategies that are unconsciously used to protect a person from anxiety arising from unacceptable thoughts or feelings."

We all use our fallback positions when we are anxious, stressed, angry, sad, or triggered. You use your protectors when you are trying to cope in a difficult situation, when difficult emotions pop up, and/or when your sense of yourself has been challenged in some way. It's not that your fallback position is all bad, but at some point it works against you.

When your fallback position (protector) interferes with your daily life (socially or physically) to the degree that it puts you at risk or damages your success or relationships, then it is a problem. You are using it to try to help you maneuver through a difficult or stressful situation, but if the end result is a more negative or problematic outcome, then it's not working for you.

Remember, these were created at a young age and you are often not even aware you are using them at the time. They are learned early in life and are taken on in order to cope with the various situations in your childhood. But since they work against you, you need to be aware of them so you can change them.

> Let's Identify Your Fall Back Positions (Protectors):
>
> Think back to some childhood frustrations. Write down how you coped with those frustrations.
> _____
> _____
> _____
>
> Here is a list of additional protectors: (put a checkmark by yours)
> ____ clings ____ withdraws ____ sacrifices ____ detaches ____ hides
> ____ competes ____ manipulates ____ isolates ____ rebels ____ argues
> ____ conforms ____ controls ____ pursues ____ criticizes ____ cuts off
> ____ complains ____ people-pleases ____ acts out
> ____ other from list above (_____) ____ other (_____)

Hot spots (triggers) are what others do that get a reaction from you. Your fallback position is what you do to protect yourself and manage the upset. Interestingly, one person's trigger can be another person's protector. When I work with couples, I always point out how their triggers and protectors play out negatively in their relationship until they bring this to their awareness. Then I help them to play out the pattern differently. Again, I'm not going to leave you stuck here. Later on I will go over what are called the higher defenses, the protectors that will lead to more successes in your life and relationships.

Once you know why you think the way you think, what makes you act the way you act, and why you react the way you react, you truly know who you are.

The most important step in all of this is knowing this about yourself so you can stop working so hard to not get the results you truly want.

You've got to do a self-assessment. You've got to ask yourself, "Does how I'm doing, thinking, reacting work?"

If what you do, how you think, and how you react works for you, then stick with it. But if it leaves you exhausted and without the results you want, then it doesn't work and you are working too hard at doing the wrong things.

And I would stop doing, thinking, and reacting that way. The way you stop is by getting control of those things. You can't control them if you don't know what they are.

Too many people just say, "Control yourself." But control what? You can't control yourself if you don't know what you need to control.

The first step is to know yourself. You've got to take this step. And that's what we've done here.

Now that you know who you are and know what can set you off and how you react and why you think the way you think, it's time to learn to control yourself. You cannot control what you do not know or cannot see.

The whole idea is not to make it more complicated, but to make it simpler and to change your results.

If what you are doing works, keep doing it. If it doesn't, pay attention here.

And that's where we are going next.

CHAPTER 4

You've Got to Control Yourself Before You Can Create Who You Want to Be—Part 1

You've done a self-assessment; you know yourself now. You realize that what you've been doing doesn't work for you. You know you've been trying to get your needs met in ways that just aren't working and letting unhelpful ways of thinking about yourself get in your way. And you see that the way you handle difficult situations works against you. You know it's time to stop doing all that you are doing that is making you work harder and still not getting you what you want.

Now it's time to get in control of those things. Now that you know what it is, you can control it.

When you are messing up and working too hard and not getting what you want, people will often tell you "just control yourself." Until you've done the first step and understood yourself, though, you don't know exactly what you need to get in control.

> You cannot control what you do not know or cannot see.

You cannot control what you do not know or cannot see. I've spent twenty-five years helping people figure out who they are and why they are that way. Then I help them to know how to change it. The first step is by learning how to control themselves.

How do you get in control?

First let's understand what's happening in your brain and body when you act in out-of-control ways.

We all have a part of our brain that helps to protect us, that keeps us safe and makes sure we survive. It's the part of the brain that judges if we are safe or not. Some people call this the caveman brain, the hind brain, the primal brain, or the emotional brain. It is an instinctual part of us.

This part of our brain is very quick to react. If our brain senses that we are in danger, it sends messages to our glands that excrete adrenaline and cortisol so we can move into action and get out of harm's way. When a bear is chasing you, that's good. When your spouse forgot to take the garbage out, it's not so good.

Simply put, if a bear is running toward you, your brain says, "I'm going die!" The feeling of fear kicks in, and that helps you to quickly get your gun or run (fight-or-flight).

That's good if a bear is running toward you. It's not so good in modern-day society. It's not so good when your spouse, or your kids, or your boss just said or did something that pisses you off.

If you want to stop working so hard at not getting what you want, then stop giving in to your instinctual reactions! (Unless a bear is running after you, of course).

Actions and Reactions

We all do many actions throughout our day. You make thousands of choices every day. You decide what clothes to wear, what route to take to work, what food you will eat for dinner, and so on.

We all struggle when we encounter stressful or difficult situations. We especially react when the situation rubs up against those core wounds and hot spots from our childhood.

For example, if you have a wound around not feeling important and someone does or says something that makes you feel unimportant, then this would be a trigger for you. It is then that the choice you make and therefore the action you take becomes imperative—because acting, or reacting, in these situations is where we often negatively impact ourselves and our relationships.

Reactions are just that—they are a **re**-action, meaning you are taking an action based on some experience from your past (recent or distant). As you learned earlier, your core unmet need(s) and limiting beliefs all came from the meanings you put on things from your past. When something happens in your present that triggers these past thoughts, feelings and experiences, then you react.

The saying goes, "Actions speak louder than words." Your actions say everything about you. What you do in various situations speaks of who you are. When you act, it can be a choice rather than an unconscious reaction.

In order to control yourself and make choices that work for you, you must learn how to control your emotions and the thoughts that accompany them so you can choose your actions wisely.

How to Control Your Feelings

When you allow your feelings and emotions to control you, you will always end up working way too hard and still not get the results you want.

- Emotions make a lousy partner.
- Emotions make a lousy parent.

- Emotions make a lousy employee.
- Emotions make a lousy financial coach.
- Emotions make a lousy nutritionist.

Every person I have worked with who has followed their emotions and allowed those emotions to control them has either ruined their lives or their relationships—or at minimum gotten the opposite of what they truly wanted in that situation. And that includes me too. I bet it includes you too!

When you allow yourself to react emotionally every time your spouse says or does "the wrong thing," you either end up in a fight, or you just stop talking all together and eventually fall out of love.

When you constantly yell at your kids, you emotionally harm them and push them further away from you. You also miss the opportunity to teach them something so that they become happy, successful adults.

When you let your emotions get in the way at work, you may get fired, or at the very least you will not be taken seriously.

When you make health and financial decisions from your emotions, you'll most likely end up fat and broke.

It's not that our emotions aren't necessary. They are. They tell us a lot. But what you do with your emotions either works for you or against you.

So then, what is the true purpose of your emotions?

Emotions compel you to take action.

However, you become your own worst enemy when you believe that the emotions you are experiencing give you permission to act out how you are feeling.

You don't want your emotions to rule if you want to have a deep, loving intimate relationship, raise happy, productive kids, enjoy a successful career, have money in the bank, and experience health and vitality.

Here are four things you can do to get in control of your feelings and emotions:

1. Go to the bathroom—really, I mean it!

If you are overwhelmed by your feelings, walk away. Excuse yourself and go to the bathroom. No one will stop you from going to the bathroom. I tell this to every client I work with.

Before you get into an argument, just go to the bathroom. I know this sounds silly, so let me tell you why I recommend this. When you go to the bathroom, you can cool off. Use this anytime. Going to the bathroom allows time for your emotions to drop. You are able to focus on something else, like washing your hands. You can look in the mirror and ask yourself, "Is this who I really want to be?" When you see your face, you can ask yourself, "Why do I look so pissed off?" or "Why am I crying?" You can then change your facial expression. When you go to the bathroom, you look in the mirror and get to **REFLECT!** You get to reflect on the way you've just been, the way you are, and the way you are about to re-enter the situation. You can ask, "Is this who I really want to be?" At least in the bathroom you can calm yourself down and start to think differently about the situation before going back into it.

There is a reason why we give kids a time-out. There is a reason why therapists teach couples the importance of taking a time-out. The bottom line is that when you have a physiological reaction to a particular situation, your heart is racing, your pulse rate is up, and you and your brain are in no condition to remain in any kind of conversation. You *will* end up saying and doing things you will regret later.

When I worked with the group home staff and with foster parents, this was always the most important thing to get across to them—because kids can really piss us off. But if you want to be a good role model for your kids, you *must* learn to walk away and calm yourself down first.

At the Gottman Institute (a world-renowned institute for couples research and therapy), they teach their couples the same thing. To help couples understand when they are physiologically flooded, they have each person wear a pulse oximeter that beeps when their pulse is at 100 beats per minute. Because we all know that our partner can really piss us off too!

Get it? It is imperative that you learn to walk away when you are in a reactive mode. Nothing good will ever come of staying in the fight.

So *use self-appointed time-outs* wisely. Anytime your feelings escalate, your wisest choice, whenever possible, is to take a time-out.

If you are in a romantic relationship, you should always set up a rule that either person can take a time-out, for a given amount of time before returning. In professional relationships when it may not be appropriate to verbally call a time-out, give yourself a way out by excusing yourself to the bathroom.

If you are on the phone or texting someone and start feeling upset, just STOP. Use a time-out. I can't tell you the number of times people have described to me the texting battles they have been in. Sometimes they will even read their texts to me, sharing what each person said while having a fight via text. Remember it's technology, and you get to be in control. Walk away. If you are on the phone or texting, just say "I'll get back to you." And then go to the bathroom!

You can walk away from most situations. If it is absolutely impossible to get away, use relaxation techniques in the moment that aren't as obvious.

And that is the second step to getting in control of your feelings.

2. Calm Yourself.

In order to really get this down and be successful at controlling yourself, it is imperative for you to learn some ways to calm your mind and body. This is where relaxation techniques can come in quite handy.

Just like learning to ride a bike, you've got to practice until it finally gets locked into your body. These are skills that must be practiced to be learned. You want to train your body and mind to shift into a calm state.

Learning to use calming techniques takes practice because when our brain and body has gone into override thinking, we are in danger of going into that fight-flight-freeze mode.

Here is the bottom line on this: Though we are greatly advanced in many ways from the caveman days, our bodies still function in the same ways. When we see a saber-toothed tiger coming our way, our body kicks into survival mode, various chemicals flood out, and we shift into fight-flight-freeze mode. We think, *I'd better fight, I'd better run, or I'd better play dead.* The problem today is that we have many stressful situations that aren't the equivalent of saber-toothed tigers. Sometimes they may feel like it, but they really aren't. For true life and death situations, such as a tornado heading for you, what your body does is helpful in order to ensure that you survive. However, for most stressful situations, such as verbal attacks by your spouse, boss, co-worker, friend, or family member, what your body does can actually get in your way. That's why, whenever possible, take a break and get away from the person and situation that has caused you to go into that danger mode. If you can't get away, at least go inside your mind and focus on a calming technique. When you have practiced this enough, your body and mind will be able to quickly get to that relaxed state.

When I work with my clients and introduce calming techniques, I explain two things. First, it is best to practice every day, at times when you aren't upset, so you can teach your mind and body what to do. Second, all the calming techniques are used to stop the negative, chattering part of your brain because as long as you are listening to that chatter, you will not be able to calm yourself down.

There is so much scientific proof today about the ability of utilizing calming techniques and their ability to change your brain chemistry in a positive way. Therefore, knowing how to utilize calming techniques can help you to quickly alter your brain chemistry so some of the flooding chemicals and hormones are reduced, thus allowing you to think more clearly before taking action. When your brain is flooding, your thinking brain is not working!

One clearly proven calming technique is deep breathing.

Breathing Techniques

There are many, many different breathing techniques out there.

First, you must make sure you are breathing correctly. Most of us, when we don't think about our breathing, are doing it correctly, from our diaphragm. But often, as soon as we start concentrating on it, we bring our breathing up to our chest. So you have to make sure you are doing deep belly or diaphragm breathing. Place your hand on or slightly above your belly button, close your eyes, and breathe in deeply and out. As you breathe in, your hand will rise (because your lungs are filling up), and as you breathe out your hand will drop (because your lungs are emptying out).

The simplest technique when it comes to breathing techniques is to breathe in and out for a set count. You can come up with a number that works for you. For example breathe in for the count of five, then breathe out to the count of six, pushing all the air out. Practice this when you are not upset. Practice for five to ten minutes at a time. Then when you are upset, it will come more easily to you. Also, the more upset you are, the better to give yourself more time to do the deep breathing. However, practicing some is better than nothing.

When I worked with foster children, I would use a plastic cup to teach this technique. I'd have them lie down on their back, place the plastic cup on their belly, and have them watch the cup raise and lower. Then I would instruct their foster parents to have the entire family lying on the living room floor with a timer set for ten minutes and practice every night. It worked! The foster children learned to calm themselves down. And you can too. Try it.

Progressive Muscle Relaxation

Progressive Muscle Relaxation is a technique created by an American physician, Edmund Jacobson, in the 1920s. We are often tense in various situations and are not even aware that our muscles are constricted. Think about driving in rush hour traffic with your hands on the wheel and then, when you get off the highway, you shift your hands and realize it hurts a little to move them because you had been holding them so tensely in the same position. This technique is actually designed to methodically tense and relax different body parts. This helps bring attention to any areas you may be tensing, but more importantly, it will help you to create relaxation throughout your body. The most important takeaway from the exercise is to focus on and note the difference between the tense and relaxed feelings in each body part as you complete it.

There are a couple of ways to do this exercise. One is to do it progressively. Start with one foot, tense and hold for about five seconds, and then relax it. Next progress up your body. Include both your right and left sides, tensing and relaxing each muscle group all the way up to your head. A second way to do it is to tense your entire body all at once and then relax it all at once. Do this several times. I am aware that in some situations (work, meetings, etc.) you may not be able to get away and do this, so you can choose just one inconspicuous body part (one hand under the table, or even your butt muscles) and just tense and relax those muscles.

Try it and see if you like it. Some people who are more in their body really like it, and others don't like it at all.

Mindfulness Techniques

There are so many mindfulness techniques. At its heart, a mindfulness technique gets you into the present moment.

When I teach with my clients a few of my favorite mindfulness techniques, I explain to them that our brain is like a giant funnel taking in billions of bits of information per second. As it takes in all these bits of information, it determines what it needs to pay attention to, and it dismisses all the rest. Sitting in my office, we are in a safe situation; the brain says, "There is nothing dangerous to worry about, so I will pay attention to what Debbie is saying." But if a large black spider suddenly was crawling on the wall, your brain (and mine too!) would move all its focus to that spider. Otherwise, if all is safe in the room, the mind dismisses a lot of information such as the picture on the wall, the lamp behind you, or the feeling of your fingers touching and the weight of your hands on your lap. Just hearing this, suddenly your brain puts the focus on your fingers touching and weight on your lap. Get it? That's mindfulness. It's not about attention per se; it's about present focus.

The main things our mind funnels out has to do with our five senses. If we are in a safe situation, we don't have to worry about the sensation of the clothes against our skin, the items we see in the room around us, the noises we hear, or the smells we smell.

Here are two of my favorite mindfulness techniques; try them—I think you will like them.

> *Body Scan* – Sit comfortably, and starting at your feet, slowly focus on the sensations of your feet against the ground, the sensation of your socks and shoes touching your feet, your pants touching your calf and shin. If your legs are crossed, feel the weight of your leg, feel the cushion below your thighs and bottom, feel the weight of your arms where they rest, the feeling of your shirt where it rests on your wrist or arms and where it touches on your torso, the sensations of your collar around your neck, your hair where it touches your face or neck, and the cushion behind your back. That's a body scan. Just quietly focus on the sensation on touch.

> *Three Senses* – Quiet yourself and identify in your head three things you hear, three things you see, and three things you feel (sensation of touch) on your body.

Pretty great, huh? If you do these exercises regularly, they will train your brain to calm quickly and get into the present moment.

Meditation and Guided Imagery

Meditation and guided imagery are two additional ways to create a relaxing state within your body. These techniques may not be able to be used on the spot for a difficult or stressful situation, but they are still worth mentioning as a way to care for yourself and reduce the constant noise and stress of this world.

> Practice at least one of these calming techniques.
>
> Circle the one you tried.
>
> ☐ Breathing   ☐ Progressive Muscle Relaxation
>
> ☐ Body Scan   ☐ Three Senses   ☐ Meditation
>
> Describe your experience when calming yourself:
>
> _____
>
> _____
>
> _____
>
> Remember, it takes practice. So keep trying different ones and keep practicing. It will work!

3. Identify Your Feelings.

Do you know how many different feelings you have throughout the day? We have as many feelings as we have thoughts, or more. Feelings are a wonderful compass for each of us. The problem is that many of us have grown up in families in which we are taught that expressing feelings is not OK or that particular feelings are OK to express, but some are not.

The truth is that **ALL** feelings are OK. In fact, they are telling us something important in the moment. But because we learned some feelings are OK and some aren't, we have also learned to not really pay attention to feelings when they are happening, especially any of the ones we learned were not acceptable. In order to manage and control your life better, you *must* learn to recognize your feelings.

> The emotional brain was conserved for a purpose. Today, physical survival is less of a threat than it was to primitive man, but data from the emotional brain still gives us important clues to our surroundings and the actions we need to take. Ignoring

this data on purpose or because we aren't aware of it leaves us with only partial information. (Emily Sterrett, PhD, *The Science Behind Emotional Intelligence*)

You cannot manage something if you do not identify or acknowledge that it exists. So start by identifying the feeling. To help you identify your feelings, you can connect to your body and scale the intensity of your feelings.

Connecting to Your Body

Your body knows you! So often we do not pay attention to our bodies, but they are telling us everything we need to know if we would just look, listen, and pay attention. In order to start to make shifts, you first have to know what is going on in the present moment, and your body will tell you. *Just listen!*

Emily Sterret in *The Science Behind Emotional Entelligence* reminds us that "emotional signals in the brain are felt throughout the body—in the gut, in the heart, in the head, in the neck, and so on. These sensations are important signals: if we learn to read them, they will help us make decisions and initiate action."

Once you know what is going on with you, you can do what you need to do with that information. You do not have to be controlled by your triggers, your thoughts, your feelings, or your fears. Often these are the parts of you that try to take over in different situations trying to "help" you out but more often get in your way.

The first step is to tune into your body. When you are in a difficult situation, slow yourself down and identify the feeling or feelings going on. Then identify where you are holding that feeling in your body. You can even connect a color to the feeling. Just get connected to it. At first you may not be able to do it in the middle of a difficult situation. If this is the case, I suggest that you take time to do it after the situation. Eventually you will be able to connect to the feeling when you first start to feel it, and in that place you will be able to choose to consciously do things different and get the results you desire.

Intensity of Feelings

Recognizing the intensity of your feelings will help you manage them. When you can identify and then use the best word to describe the intensity of feeling, you can then scale the feeling, and this will help you to manage that feeling. If you are just a little irritated with someone, you can more easily come up with the words to communicate the irritation and express what is going on and what would be a more helpful action from them. However, if you are raging at them, your ability to manage that anger and talk rationally to them in that moment is less likely to be successful.

The English language has many different feeling words. In order to identify your feelings, it will help to use the word that best fits the intensity of it for you. For example: You are feeling sad. But is it just that you are feeling *down*, or you are feeling *sad*, or *miserable*, or *distraught*? Then, using a scale from zero to ten, you want to assign a number to the feeling. Zero means you are not feeling that feeling at all, and ten means it is the biggest, worst time you have ever felt the feeling in your ENTIRE LIFE. So identify the best word and then scale it.

As human beings when our numbers are on the higher side, we end up acting in ways that are often harmful to ourselves and our relationships, and thus we often regret our actions. So the next step when scaling is to note the number you were at when you acted out. Feel that number and feeling in your body. Then take the number down two, three, or four numbers, and that is the number (along with the feeling in your body) that you need to train yourself to pay attention to. At the lower number you can take other more helpful actions before the number gets too high. By doing this you will find yourself creating results and taking actions that make you feel better about yourself, have positive outcomes in your relationships, and ultimately help you not work so hard at getting what you don't want.

When you pay attention and manage your feelings, you will be able to make more effective decisions in the moment and get more of what you do want.

> Let's Get Connected to Your Feelings:
>
> Feelings in Your Body (Note: One feeling can be felt in more than one place)
>
> When you feel sad, where do you feel that in your body? _____
>
> When you feel mad, where do you feel that in your body? _____
>
> When you feel scared, where do you feel that in your body? _____
>
> When you feel happy, where do you feel that in your body? _____
>
> Going forward: On a regular basis, pay attention to the feelings in your body. Name the feeling. You can even identify a color that goes with the feeling. And scale the intensity of the feeling on a scale of zero to ten.

4. Get Busy.

In situations where you have more intense feelings, you may need a little more time to calm yourself. The best way to do this is to distract yourself. Get busy with something that engages your brain.

Do *not* take a time-out only to ruminate on what happened, what the other person said or did, how wrong the other person was, or justifying in your head why you did what you did. I know that is where we all want to go, and I've done it myself. We all have. But it *never* serves us to go round and round in the negative chatter.

Instead calm yourself and then get your body and brain busy with something.

> **List six things you can do that will engage your brain:**
> (a crossword puzzle, a video game, clean out a closet or a junk drawer, exercise, listen to music)
> 1) _____ 2) _____
> 3) _____ 4) _____
> 5) _____ 6) _____

Remember, we all have the brain chemistry and hormones that flood through us when we are feeling threatened (and that can include feeling emotionally threatened). When adrenaline and cortisol are flooding through us, we go to fight-flight-freeze mode. That's why recognizing and naming your feelings, noting the intensity of your feelings, and learning to take a time-out is imperative if you want to improve your relationships and stop doing what you shouldn't be doing.

All four of these steps and learning how to control your feelings are imperative. If you constantly let yourself be led from your emotional brain in an irrational place, you will never be able to get more of the results you want and stop doing what you shouldn't do. When you learn to control your feelings, you will be able to do the rest in order to get more of what you want.

Once you've practiced the skills in this chapter, you'll have learned to calm yourself and manage your feelings. In the next chapter, we'll cover what to do with crazy, negative thoughts that accompany those feelings.

CHAPTER 5

You've Got to Control Yourself Before You Can Create Who You Want to Be—Part 2

Once you've gotten control of your feelings, you can work on what to do with all the negative thoughts that came along with those feelings.

How many thoughts a day do you have? You might be surprised to learn that, in general, human beings have fifty to sixty thousand thoughts per day.

Thoughts are imperative when it comes to managing your feelings and choosing what actions to take. In other words, your thoughts can make or break you when it comes to your life, your relationships, and your happiness.

Your feelings are like a weather barometer; they are just telling you something. Your thoughts are the meanings you put on the weather, which in turn will direct what actions you take. When the barometer says it's raining, your thoughts interpret the situation and tell you that you'd better grab your umbrella.

Your thoughts are just that: *your* thoughts. They may or may not be accurate, and they may or may not be helpful. The good news is that you can **change your thoughts**. Let me give you an example. Let's say you are going to a party at your friend's house, and you are already feeling insecure about the zit on your face. You arrive, and there are lots of people at the party. You open the screen door. Your friend is talking with someone else in the corner of the room, and they both look at you, look away, and start to laugh. You feel hurt, and the thought that goes through your mind is *I thought she was my friend, but she is laughing at me.* Maybe you are rude to your friend for the rest of the night, or maybe you get depressed, eat all the appetizers, and sit by yourself the rest of evening. You might leave and go home with plans to never speak to your friend again. Or perhaps you go up to your friend and loudly accuse her of making fun of you.

Here is the question, though. Are you 100 percent sure your thought was accurate? What if, when you saw your friend laughing, you stopped, went to the bathroom, used a calming technique, identified your feeling of being hurt, recognized the initial thought that your friend was laughing at you, and then chose to change the thought. Let's say you changed the thought to *I wonder what they are laughing at that is so funny,* or *Maybe they just looked at me because I walked in the door, but they were laughing because of what they had just been talking about.* You could now go up and ask them what is so funny. You might find out that one of them had just told a funny story. By recognizing your feeling, stopping your initial thought, changing it to another possible thought, and checking it out, you were able to realize that your initial feeling of hurt was from your own stuff; that initial thought was out of your own insecurity and was, in fact, *inaccurate.* By taking this step and changing the thought, everything changed for the evening.

This is one example of how all of us do this to ourselves *all the time*! When you allow a feeling to fly by and don't take the time to identify it, you can quickly jump to a potentially inaccurate or unhelpful thought. This kind of thought can wreak havoc on you and your relationships.

The key is that you must start paying attention to your thoughts *before* you act on them. Start by training yourself to note both the thought and the feeling in a given situation before doing anything else. Ask yourself questions about the thought. Remember, the thought is your interpretation of the situation. Ask yourself if there is a possibility that you don't have the whole story. Ask yourself (whether you have the whole story or not) if this thought is helpful for you or not. By slowing down and catching your thoughts first, you will be able to take more helpful actions.

> Remember, our hind brain is there to protect us, so it automatically comes up with negative thoughts. That's what it does. It is up to us whether we believe them or not.

Remember, our hind brain is there to protect us, so it automatically comes up with negative thoughts. That's what it does. It is up to us whether we believe them or not. In *Feeling Good: The New Mood Therapy*, David Burns describes ten different ways we twist our thinking. Each person uses different ways. In general a patterned way of thinking that you consistently use may have been modeled to you by your parents.

1. All-or-Nothing Thinking: This is black-and-white thinking. "If I don't do it perfectly, I've failed."
2. Mental Filter: You only look for certain evidence, find all the negative, and ignore the positives.

3. Overgeneralizing: You see one negative event as a never-ending pattern or you are overly broad in your conclusions. "Everything always fails" or "Nothing good ever happens to me."
4. Disqualifying the Positives: You insist on discounting your accomplishments or positive qualities.
5. Jumping to Conclusions: There are two different ways you might be doing this. First, you may be mindreading—imagining in negative terms what people are thinking, or second, fortune telling—predicting the future in some way as always turning out badly.
6. Magnification or Minimization: You either blow things way out of proportion and catastrophize something or you shrink it to seem less important.
7. Emotional Reasoning: You assume because you feel a certain way, it must be true. "I'm embarrassed and feel like an idiot, so it must be true."
8. Should Statements: You consistently criticize yourself with words like *should, shouldn't, must, ought*, and *have to*. This makes you feel guilty or like you have already failed. And when you use those words on others, you are setting yourself and them up for frustration and failure too.
9. Labeling: You identify and assign a label to yourself based on your shortcomings. You make a mistake and label yourself a "loser." You can do this to others as well.
10. Personalization: You blame yourself for something that wasn't completely your fault. When you do this with others, you blame them and overlook your part in the problem.

Which of these do you primarily use?

> Let's Identify Yours:
>
> Reread the list of the ten twisted ways of thinking above and identify your top three—the ones you use the most.
>
> Write them down:
>
> 1) _____
>
> 2) _____
>
> 3) _____
>
> Now start to catch yourself when you use them.

Luckily we don't have to stay stuck in all that negative thinking. Once you start paying attention and capturing your thoughts, you can change them. And that is where reframing comes in.

Reframing

Do you really believe that you are totally in control of your thoughts? It's true—you can **change** them!

The issue is that so many of our daily thoughts are negative, either directed at ourselves or directed at others. Remember, though, thoughts are just thoughts. They have no meaning associated with them. Negative thoughts usually are tied to your core needs and your background experiences. They are actually trying to serve, protect, or help you in some way. It they are critical, they are trying to motivate you to do something different; if they are negative toward others, they are trying to protect you.

So given all that, we still can change our thoughts. We are the ones making them up in our head, so we can be in control of them.

A thought is only a story we tell ourselves, whether it is a thought in a difficult or conflictual situation, a limited belief, or even a pleasant thought. The way we work as human beings is that once we tell ourselves that story, we believe it is true. Then we set about to find proof or evidence that this story is true. If it is a negative thought, you end up reinforcing the negativity and bringing that into your life.

Let's change those negative thoughts. The idea of reframing is to consciously choose to change the way you see things (your thought about something). Once you do this, you then begin to look for the evidence to prove this story as true.

If you are going to tell yourself a story, why not tell it so it's in your favor?

In order to change your negative, twisted thinking, once you have calmed yourself down and have your rational, integrating brain working again, you must challenge those thoughts. There are many different ways you can challenge your negative thinking. The one that I have found most helpful that I teach all my clients comes from Trauma Focused Cognitive Behavioral Therapy. It is simply asking yourself "Is that thought 100 percent accurate?"

> "Is that thought 100 percent accurate?"

Get into the habit of asking yourself this question. The majority of the time, you will realize that it is not 100 percent accurate. This allows your brain to reframe and change it to a more helpful way of thinking.

When I teach this to my clients, I often share this personal story:

> I went to the doctor to get a mammogram done. As an older woman, I have had several mammograms over the years. As we all know, the technician that does the mammogram will not

tell you the results. At the end of each session, year after year, the technician says to me, "The results will come at the end of the week." I leave and go on my merry way, not thinking twice about it. By the end of the week, I receive a letter in the mail stating that the results were negative.

However, this time the technician said to me, "The doctor will be calling you by the end of the week." Now I know that if the doctor calls you, that means there is a problem, and that's where my thoughts went. I must have had a shocked look on my face when she said that, so she then said, "Or if you're lucky, maybe they will send out a letter." That didn't help me at all; it only made it worse. I left the office convinced that there was a problem. By the time I got to my car, I was ruminating on all these negative thoughts. I was telling myself I must have cancer and taking it to a dark place in my mind.

When I got into my car, I knew I needed to switch my thinking. First, I sat in my car and did some deep breathing and a body scan. Then I asked myself, "Is it 100 percent accurate that I have cancer?" Of course the answer was "no." So then I had to switch my thinking. I changed my thoughts to "Perhaps she was a new technician, and she didn't know how to end the session with the correct standard statement. I have not had any issues with any of my mammograms over all these years. My family doesn't have a history of breast cancer. I'm sure I am fine." Then I turned the radio on and started driving home. But my hind brain, which is fear-based, brought me back to the negative thoughts. I restated all my positive reframes in my head, and then I started singing to the music on the radio in order to stop the chatter in my brain. And when I got home, I worked on some projects that needed to be done so I would keep my mind busy.

I'd love to say that was the end of it, but there were a few times during the week that the fearful negative thoughts popped up again. Again I ran the positive reframes and then kept myself busy. At the end of the week, I received the letter stating all was good.

You can use the "Is it 100 percent accurate?" question in both big and small situations.

When I worked with kids and adults who have trauma in their background, it was imperative that I helped them to reframe some of the negative stories they made up during their trauma experiences. I worked with one woman who was sexually abused by her uncle (but not to the point of intercourse). Yet she told herself she was not a virgin because of what he did to her. Through a variety of questions and looking at facts about how the body works, I was able to help her to switch the story.

I regularly work with wives who complain about their husbands. I help them to see that they have created a negative story in their head around a situation. A common one is that they describe some action their spouse is doing or not doing and say, "He doesn't care about me." Then I challenge it. "So is it 100 percent accurate that he has never cared about you? He has never done any caring acts for you in your entire relationship—is that true?" Every time they laugh a little and say, "No, it's not true." Then, depending on the situation, we change it to a more helpful thought. "He does care about me and shows me when he takes the trash out to the curb every week, when he comes home from work on time, and when he kisses me goodbye every morning. I just have to let him know that it's important to me and shows me he cares when he remembers to put his clothes in the hamper too."

Get it? You can do this in all sorts of situations in your relationships—and even for any negative thoughts in day-to-day moments.

Instead of saying, "I am overwhelmed, and I will never get this done," ask yourself if that is 100 percent accurate and then change it to "I feel overwhelmed, but I will break this down step-by-step, and I will eventually get to the end."

After a disappointing experience, instead of saying, "Nothing ever works out for me," challenge it and then switch it to "This experience did not work out for me, but I will learn from it, and I know at other times things have worked out for me."

My clients who regularly catch their negative thoughts and ask themselves this question in various difficult situations are the ones who make the most progress and start creating more of what they want by changing the way they think.

Stop believing the negative stories you are telling yourself that work against you and your relationships. Regularly challenge your negative thoughts by asking "Is this 100 percent accurate?" or "Is this thought helpful for me?" And then switch to a more positive thought.

Try it—it really will work for you!

Let's Change Your Thoughts:

Think of the last upsetting situation you were in:

Identify and write down the negative thoughts that fueled the feelings.

_____
_____
_____

For example, "He left the dirty dishes in the sink again. He always does that. He knows that bothers me. He just doesn't care about me."

Challenge the negative thoughts. Ask yourself, "Is this 100 percent true?" or "Is this a helpful thought for me?"

_____

_____

_____

For example: "He did leave the dirty dishes in the sink today, but for the last three days, he didn't. He does care about me. He brought home the dry cleaning the other day."

Change the thought to a more helpful thought. It always helps to give someone the benefit of the doubt.

_____

_____

_____

For example: "He must have been really rushed this morning and didn't get to the dishes. He does so many other things for me that show he cares."

After an upsetting situation, how many times have you said to yourself, "Why did I say [or do] that?" Until you understand where those overwhelming negative feelings and thoughts come from and know how to manage them, you will continue to be powerless, controlled by them, and reactive.

> When you control yourself, when you master your emotions and negative thoughts, you will become the master of your results.

When you control yourself, when you master your emotions and negative thoughts, you will become the master of your results. You will be able to stop doing what you shouldn't do, working so hard not getting what you want, and you will start getting more of what you want in your life and relationship.

One gentleman beautifully described how he learned to know himself and control his thoughts and feelings as he was happily celebrating forty years of marriage. He shared that he knew his hot spots; he knew his fallback position was to yell, and he knew that when he was upset, he could get brutal and ugly with his words. He learned this by watching his mom and dad engage in all sorts of yelling and nasty words, but then afterward they hugged and all was good. Early on in his marriage, he discovered that did not work with his wife because her fallback position was to run and hide. The louder he yelled, the quieter she became, and then she would walk away. She would be hurt by his sharp tongue, and then he'd feel bad (even though he didn't understand why she got so hurt), and he'd spend time trying to fix her bad feelings. Finally, when he learned to walk away first and calm himself, he came up with a different way to handle things. Through the use of email, they were able to manage their conflict constructively, and they both got more of what they wanted. He learned to reframe his thoughts and temper his words through his writing, and she learned to speak up and assert herself through her writing. How ingenious!

Now it is time for you to start speaking up for yourself in ways that will actually work for you.

CHAPTER 6

You've Got to Speak Up for Yourself to Get More of What You Want

Speaking up means that you are actually using words that lift the situation up and move toward resolution so you get the results you want. And if your words don't move to resolution, *just don't say them*!

Before you speak, ask yourself, "Are these helpful words that will move us to resolution?" The faster you are able to do this assessment, the more successful you will be.

Why We Don't Speak Up
Don't ask, Don't Tell

As human beings we don't ask for what we really want and we don't say what we are really thinking. Why? Why don't we speak up for ourselves?

We've got to go back to our caveman brain to answer this question.

Our caveman brain is about survival and safety. When that part of our brain turns its focus on the people around us, fear often sets in.

What if I tell my spouse what I'm really thinking? They might get mad. They might think I'm weird. They might reject me. They might say no.

If I tell my employee what they are doing wrong or what I want them to do differently, they might quit, and then where will I be?

If I ask my business partner to dress more professionally, he might get mad, and it will be uncomfortable in the office or it may end the partnership.

If I ask my teenage daughter to clean her room, she will get mad and sulk and make things miserable in the house.

If I tell my adult son that lives in another state that I'd like us to talk more often, he might get upset, and then I'll end up talking to him even less often.

If I say something, I will only make it worse.

So we don't speak up. We don't ask for what we want, and we certainly don't become vulnerable and share what's really on our mind, until . . .

someone really pisses us off.

To Power Struggle or Not to Power Struggle?

Once our caveman brain feels threatened, it will often move into fight mode.

This is where bad conflict sets in, the circular kind where nothing gets resolved. The kind where both people get uglier and uglier with their words and tone.

You say something that pushes my button, and I go into fight mode. I say something that pushes your button, so you notch it up and say something back, and round and round it goes—until it gets so loud that the neighbors call the police or one person threatens to end the relationship. It never ends well.

In bad conflict, we don't really hear or understand each other, and the worst parts of us tend to come out. All we know is that we are right, and we are determined to get the other person to see that. At some point the fight may end, but nothing has been resolved. We are left with relationship damage and disconnect.

Or we may be dealing with someone that moves more into avoidance mode (flight), and we end up living through hours or even days of silence with each other.

I worked with one woman whose husband was so angry with her that they went six weeks without talking to each other. Could you imagine, six weeks living in the same home and not talking to each other! Wow! They slept in separate rooms. He'd run upstairs as soon as he heard her car entering the garage (she knew because she'd see the lights in the house shift), and when he was home, he'd even keep his office door locked so she couldn't come in. It finally ended only when she served him with divorce papers. At that point he agreed to get into his own therapy, and they began couples therapy. But they had a long way to go to learn how to hear each other and manage conflict in a way that moved to resolution.

The problem with bad conflict is that we are working from our caveman brain, and it becomes a power struggle. You against me—someone needs to win and someone needs to lose.

Power struggles never resolve anything.

No one likes to feel like another person is wielding power over them. Pretty much from two years old on, we fight against someone else having power over us.

But when you step out of a power struggle, it changes everything.

In the case of one couple I worked with, the husband used to tell his wife what she could or couldn't do. Sometimes she would go along with it just to keep the peace. But there would always be resentment afterward that would usually come out in some sort of spiteful action. She wouldn't talk to him or she wouldn't do something around the house that she usually would do. Sometimes she'd just do whatever he told her not to do, and then he'd get mad at her and they'd spend a few days in silence. This was their pattern for nineteen years!

One session, after they had shifted their relationship and were both doing the simple practices I had taught them, he told me that now he spent time thinking about what and how to say something to her in ways that are more helpful. During the coronavirus safe-at-home time, she had a trip planned to visit her adult son in a different state. Her husband was worried because she still was planning to go on the trip. On two separate occasions, he gently asked if she thought it would be safe, and he shared his concern. She thought about it and made her own decision to postpone the trip. He laughed and said that in the past he would have just told her she couldn't go. When I asked her about it, she told me how different this was and how it created a feeling of connection with him rather than separation. Now she knew it came from a place of concern and love, not of lording power over her.

So learn to step out of power struggles because someone will always lose. And ultimately that means you and the relationship you value will fail.

We don't speak up because we are afraid of the other person's response or reaction AND because we don't know how to do it in a way that brings resolution. Therefore it always ends in ugly conflict. Once again, we are working too hard and still not getting the results we desire.

What Can You Do?

Sadly most of us are not taught how to communicate effectively. We are not taught in school, and we most certainly are not taught by our parents or other adults around us when we are children. So usually when we attempt to step into difficult conversations, we blow it. We either don't speak up in a clear enough way that the other person understands what we are saying, or we criticize and accuse the other person, thinking they will actually hear what we are saying. But no one likes to be told what they are doing wrong or what they should do. At other times we just avoid it all together, allowing our resentment and eventual contempt for the other person to grow. In any and all cases, we work way too hard only to get devastating results.

So how good are you at getting the message you want across to another person?

Are you really pushy about your position? Do you sit back and let the other person control the conversation and decide everything? Do you try to see how to work together or do you dig in your heels and stick to your position? Are you unwilling to work with the other person's thoughts or ideas? The most productive way to succeed in conflict is to keep an attitude of wanting to work together in order to work things out. At the same time, you want to hold your position without forcing it on the other person, and you want to be open and curious about their position.

There are specific things you can do to make sure you are actually heard when you do speak up. It's all about your attitude and **the way you approach it**, **the way you listen,** and **the way you speak up**.

Following are effective communication skills that will help you to be better heard and understood.

The Way You Approach It

It's all in the way you think about conflict long before you speak up that will set things going in the right direction. Here are five ways you can approach conflict that will make things easier and help conflict to have a positive outcome.

Start with the right mindset.

If you want to actually be heard, then you must approach a difficult conversation with the attitude of "It's you and me against the problem." This mindset will help you and your relationship.

Think about it: When you feel under attack because of a criticism or accusation, you automatically shift to a stance of you against the other person. You begin to defend yourself and attack the other person. This always creates more hurt and damage in the relationship. So first take a time-out and calm yourself. Then once you are calm, shift your mindset to "It's you and me against the problem."

> "It's you and me against the problem."

I know it's easier said than done. But do it! It will change everything. I worked with one couple that actually posted this several places in their house to help remind them when they were upset. They successfully shifted how they managed conflict.

Give them the benefit of the doubt.

Remember that in general people aren't out to get us. Most often the people we are in relationships with just get caught up in what they are thinking or doing. They don't purposely mean to hurt us or let us down.

> "My teenager doesn't hate me. She's just being a teenager and needs her own space."

"I am important to my husband. He was just excited about buying his new computer that's why he forgot I asked him to help me clean the house. He'll help me when he comes back."

"I know our friendship is important because she planned my birthday party last year. I know she's just been busy dealing with her son getting ready to go off to college. That's why she hasn't reached out to me for a while."

"My business partner has been grumpy lately, but I know he has a lot of stress in his family life right now."

After years of negative patterns in a relationship, we often begin to interpret everything the other person does as negative, and we stop giving them the benefit of the doubt. John Gottman calls this Negative Sentiment Override. This can be turned around with a lot of direct focus on appreciation and fondness work. But it is a lot easier to give them the benefit of the doubt and to speak up effectively early on in the relationship so these bad patterns don't become established.

Acknowledge what they have done well.

In your mind ahead of time as well as when you start the conversation, acknowledge the positives about the other person. Think about and then share something they did about the situation you are bringing up or something else they did that you appreciate.

Research has shown that couples that are more successful during conflict have a 5:1 ratio of seeing and speaking to the positive the other person is doing versus the negative. That research has been shown to be true in schools as well. When teachers praise and comment on what kids do well with a 5:1 ratio, kids are more successful. This research has been repeated in businesses as well; when employees feel appreciated and acknowledged for what they do well, they are happier and more productive at work.

Remember to use the question "Is that 100 percent accurate?" to help you to remember that your upset thought means you are forgetting the whole picture. Find the positives in the other person and in their actions. That will help the conversation to go better because the other person will feel acknowledged for what they have done well, and it will make them more open to what you have to say.

Be self-aware.

Be aware of your nonverbal communication skills. This includes your tone of voice, facial expression, and body language. Albert Mehrabian from UCLA completed a study and wrote a book called *Simple Messages*. He discovered that the meaning behind what someone is communicating comes from:

- 55 percent facial expression
- 38 percent tone of voice
- 7 percent words

This is important for you to understand because clearly, our words are not all that is being heard. All of our nonverbal expressions are packaged along with our words in any situations in which we communicate.

Some nonverbals to keep in mind when you are communicating include eye contact, facial expressions, body posture, distance apart, energy level, voice speed and volume, intensity.

Make sure your nonverbals match your words. Otherwise people's caveman brains will read the nonverbals over your words and will not trust what you are saying.

If you are too emotional to communicate to someone in a way that your verbal and nonverbals match, you need to take a time-out, calm yourself down, and deal with your stuff. Only then will you be able to be effective in talking with someone else. Pay attention to your feelings.

Check in with your thoughts. Pay attention to your body and your breathing. You must be able to manage your own stress and potentially out-of-control feelings. If you are breathing shallow and quickly, slow your breathing. If you are speaking loudly, lower your voice.

If your emotions are too intense, you must soothe and calm yourself first. DO NOT go into a conversation if you are not calm first and DO NOT stay in a conversation if you get escalated or if the other person gets escalated. It will never end well.

Ask permission/set a good time.

No one likes to be ambushed. Make sure you start by asking if it's a good time to talk. If they say "yes," great. If they say "no," schedule a time that works for both of you.

And better still, for your significant other relationship, set a weekly time to check in on how the relationship is going.

The Way You Listen

Believe it or not, the next step to speaking up is learning to *listen* first. When you listen first, it creates all sorts of good stuff that moves toward connection and resolution. It helps you to understand the other person. When the other person feels understood, they are more open to understanding your perspective. It creates a safer experience for both of you, and in a safe place you can be more vulnerable, open, and honest. All of that creates a deeper connection, which is what we all want—understanding and connection. Below are four ways to learn to become a better listener.

1. Be an active listener first.

We all tend to focus on ourselves in our relationships. "What does he think of **ME**?" "**I** hope they liked what **I** did." We tend to run things in our mind around what they have to do with us. We especially do this when we are upset or have been hurt in some way by someone else. We then focus on ourselves, our experience of the situation, our feelings, and our thoughts. We usually do this because we go into a protective mode.

Have you found yourself in a conversation, and as the person was talking, you were thinking about how you were going to respond to what they were saying? We all do that. In order to have deeper, successful conversation you need to bring active listening skills into your relationships. This means you will need to make a conscious effort to get out of your head so you can be present and focus on the other person.

Stay out of your own mind, don't interrupt, let the other person know you are listening with *uh-huhs* and *hmms*, and keep an open mind.

Here is a trick to help you: Have a paper and pen available during a potentially difficult conversation. When you think of something you want to say to defend yourself, write it down. Your brain can then let it go so you can keep listening. When it's your turn, you can come back to what you have written down.

2. Use gentle words.

When I work with couples to help them with better conflict management, I ask them, "What do you do at work when your boss or co-worker pisses you off?" Most people say they manage it somehow. They walk away or they respond in a professional way. Then I ask them, "Do you love your boss or co-worker?" They laugh and say no. Then I ask, "So you speak respectfully at work, but when it comes to the people you love most—your kids or your spouse—you speak in unkind, disrespectful ways?" That always gets them to stop in their tracks and rethink.

I know that at work we have a deeper fear of losing our job, and that connects to our survival instinct. With our loved ones we can let ourselves be hurt more easily and react. But it is just as important in your personal relationships to manage your words.

The bottom line is: be respectful, use kind, gentle words, and practice good manners such as saying "please" and "thank you" in all of your encounters. Think before you say something. Slow yourself and the conversation down. Ask yourself, "How would I feel if that were said to me?" If you don't want it said to you, don't say it to someone else.

3. *Mirror, validate, and empathize.*

Mirroring is just a fancy word for paraphrasing what the other person says. Make sure you capture what they say, not your interpretation of what they are saying.

Validation is the ability to find something you can acknowledge that supports a person's truth and perspective. If you can't agree with most of what they say, you can at least validate how they are feeling. Remember, everyone has a right to their own feelings.

Empathy is the ability to step into another person's shoes and connect to the way they are feeling

Putting these three together would look something like: "What I hear you saying is that you felt embarrassed when I made a negative comment about your outfit in front of my parents (mirror). As I think about it, it makes sense to me that you felt embarrassed (validate); I would have felt the same way if you had done that to me in front of your parents (empathy)."

4. *Be compassionate and curious.*

Get out of being right and get into having compassion and being curious about what is going on for the other person.

Every one of us wants to be understood; we want others to hear and agree with our perspective. During conflict, though, your caveman brain gets stuck on thinking you need to defend yourself. So you end up believing you have to get the other person to understand and accept your point of view. But the opposite is actually true. Instead of insisting that the other person understand you, start with the desire to understand the other person. We all experience hurt, pain, and misunderstanding, and we all long for understanding, love, and connection.

When conflict arises, remind yourself to be compassionate and curious first. Compassion and curiosity will move you toward deeper connection. So manage your own feelings and thoughts, shift to the position of "you and me against the problem," put your perspective temporarily on the shelf, and be compassionate and curious toward the other person. Connection isn't in being right, winning, or getting the other person to give up their viewpoint. Connection is made when you can step into the other person's perspective so that deeper understanding is created. Therefore, go into the conversation with compassion and curiosity.

Ask curious, clarifying questions such as:

- "Help me to understand what you were feeling."
- "Tell me what you were thinking."
- "Help me understand what you mean by this."
- "Then what happened?"
- "What else is going through your mind about this?" "How did this all start?"
- "What do you think is happening for you that has triggered this?"
- "Where in your past have you felt this way?"

The Way You Speak Up

State your fear up front.

If the conversation you are about to have is making you anxious because you are worried about the other person's reaction, it can help to state your fear up front.

- "What I don't want is for you to think that I am mad at you."
- "I'm afraid that when I bring this topic up, you will get upset but it's important we talk about it."

State what you hope to accomplish in the conversation.

- I need you to hear and acknowledge me.
- I hope you will be able to acknowledge your part in this too.
- I want us to problem-solve around the issue.
- I'm hoping we can come to a compromise.
- I need reassurance.
- I'm hoping for an apology once you understand my perspective.

Be clear and concise.

Don't go on and on and on. No one can track everything you say when you go on and on. Enough said.

Use "I" statements.

We have probably all heard of "I" statements at some time in our life. But if we haven't been taught how to do them, we usually turn them around into "you" statements.

The reason "I" statements work is that we are sharing about our feelings and thoughts, and we do not criticize the other person. When someone feels criticized, their caveman brain automatically goes on the defense.

However, "I" statements makes us feel vulnerable. It is difficult to share our feelings, and most of us have not been taught to share them.

In working with children who have been victims of abuse, after working through their trauma and helping them to process and make sense of it, I then move into communication skills so they can feel empowered. Statistically children who have been victimized commonly become victims later in their adult life. So learning to speak up in effective ways is important for these kids. And it's important for us too.

I role-play with these children and have them practice saying "no" loudly. I then teach them to state what they feel and what they need. We role-play different scenarios in their family, at school, and with their friends.

- "I'm feeling scared; I need to talk to you."
- "I'm feeling mad; I need to take a time out."
- "I'm feeling frustrated; I need you to stop."
- "I'm feeling sad; I need a hug."

Simple, right? I want them to speak up, and I want you to speak up too. This is what an "I" statement looks like:

"I felt _____ (use actual feeling words like *sad, disappointed, upset*, etc.)
when you _____ (only describe the actual facts)
because _____ (explain the meaning you tied to that feeling and/or their behavior),
and what I want/need is _____ (be specific)."

For example:

"I feel resentful when you leave your dishes in the sink because it seems like you expect me to do them; in the future I would like you to put your dishes in the dishwasher."

Saying "I" statements will not feel comfortable at first, but the more you do it, the easier it will become. Using "I" statements can make a positive difference in any situation.

Make a positive request—don't demand.

It's worth emphasizing here: The fourth part of the "I" statement works best when it states a positive need. It is so easy for us to come up with what we want people to stop doing. But that typically comes across as though they are doing something wrong, and that puts them on the defense.

Think first and change the negative "stop doing this" to a positive "start doing this."

Also keep in mind that you have the right to request a different action or behavior, but you don't have the right to demand that the other person does it. The other person has the right to say yes or no to your request. Then they can tweak your request to an action they can actual follow through on.

In the above example, the response to the request could be "I will do my best, and when I don't have time, I will let you know I was unable to do it on that night."

Be proactive and keep them informed.

We all have our own internal dialogue. We jump to conclusions and fill in the gaps about others all the time.

Therefore, the more proactive you are at keeping the other person informed of your plans, thoughts, and expectations, the better things will go and the fewer conflicts you'll have.

A client described a conflict that occurred between her and her mother. It was finals week at school, and she had a paper that had to get done. Her mother wanted to get the garage cleaned out before the family came to visit. They had begun working on the garage and then her mom got pulled away to do something, so my client decided it was a good time to work on her paper. When her mother came back and saw she wasn't working on the garage, she became upset and began yelling at my client, telling her she was being lazy and not carrying her weight in the household. As we discussed what happened, we brainstormed that she could have left a simple note for her mom stating, "I know you want the garage worked on. I'm going to my room for one hour to work on my school paper, and then I'll be back to work on the garage." We agreed that this could have drastically changed the direction of that incident.

One person I was talking to said it perfectly: "Don't leave room for interpretation." As human beings, our brain likes to fill in the gaps. So be proactive, keep others informed, and fill in the gaps accurately first before their mind fills them in inaccurately.

Let's Practice Speaking Up:

Think of something you have been wanting to speak up about but have either avoided or already blew it and said it poorly.

Change it into an "I" statement:

I felt _____

when you

_____

_____

because

_____

_____

What I need/want

_____

_____

Now go try it out.

Conflict is a normal part of relationships. But it doesn't have to end in despair, hurt, or anger. Deeper connection is possible when you are willing to look at and understand the way you control yourself, hold the mindset of "you and me against the problem," and learn to consistently speak up in ways that will actually work.

The way you approach conflict, the way you listen, and the way you speak up will all help you to do more of what you should do so that you get more of what you want. Mastering these skills will work for you. I've seen it over and over again, and it works for me too.

> "We all need a witness to our lives." (from the movie *Shall We Dance*)

Susan Sarandon's character in *Shall We Dance* said, "We all need a witness to our lives. . . . Your life will not go unnoticed because I will notice it. Your life will not go unwitnessed because I will be your witness."

We all desire to be heard. The way to do that is to speak up for yourself in ways that move to resolution and connection.

When people are feeling heard and seen, a deeper connection is made and happiness and relationship success are increased.

Knowing yourself, controlling yourself, and finally speaking up for yourself will get you the results you want. But in order for it all to work, you must stand up for yourself. **It's time to put all this into action!**

CHAPTER 7

You've Got to Stand Up for Yourself to Get More of What You Want

Now it's time to take all that we have talked about and put it into action!

In order to get the results you want, you must take all your self-awareness, self-control, and ability to speak up for yourself and tie these to your actions.

When you truly speak up for yourself, your actions must follow. To speak up also means to stand up. You must put actions with the words, or all that you have learned up to this point won't mean a thing.

But remember, it doesn't make sense to do the actions if those actions don't get you what you want.

Will my actions move towards resolution? Will my actions move me toward the results I want? The faster you are able to do this assessment, the more successful you will be.

It's taking action that counts!

> It's taking action that counts!

She came to me because her husband had just found out about her prior affair. She was a mess. They were a mess. First, we worked on how she needed to take full responsibility for her actions and what to do and say to her husband during this crisis time. Then I began to help her to really look at herself. In the beginning she wanted to blame the affair on what was happening in their marriage: she fought with him about the kids, about how much time he spent at his parent's house, about not spending time with her, and so on. Once she understood that it was about her and her needs that led her to cheat on him and she learned to better control her emotions and reactions, she was then able to offer her husband a heartfelt, honest apology for her actions. Next I coached her on knowing how to address her concerns and speak up and ask for what she wanted. Finally she began to take the helpful actions toward rebuilding a stronger relationship with her spouse.

All seemed great—and for the relationship it was. Around eight months into our work together, she shared a current stress she was experiencing at work. I listened and supported her in all her feelings and experiences, but as I listened, I saw a similar pattern. I said to her, "Don't let yourself get dragged down in the muck and the mire of the messiness that's going on there. This is what you did with the situation with your husband, too, and it led you to cheating. Be proactive and empower yourself, speak up, and stand up for yourself." We were able to create a plan for what she could say to her boss, and how she might find another place to work as well.

This is a perfect example of what we all do at times. We sit in the muck and mire. We sit in the messiness too long, and it leads us to taking wrong actions. When we aren't aware of our "stuff" that comes up in particular situations, when we allow ourselves to stay in negative emotions and negative thoughts, when we go into "poor me" mode, we end up doing something that makes the situation worse.

When was the last time you stayed in the muck and mire and ended up doing something that worked against you? Maybe it wasn't as messy as an affair, but I bet what you did made the situation worse.

It's only when you stand up for yourself and take the right actions that you will be able to stop working harder than you need to and therefore get more of what you want.

Now that you know who you are, can control your negative feelings and thoughts, and know how to effectively speak up for yourself, it's time to put all that into action.

What Does Standing Up for Yourself Look Like?

Take responsibility. It always starts with you. You cannot change something if you don't acknowledge your part in the situation. You must start by taking responsibility. This means that you look at yourself and own your part in the situation. It means that you apologize for your impact. It means that you correct what you can. It's not always the most comfortable thing, but there is a sense of relief once you have taken responsibility. Now you can learn, grow, and make changes.

This is at the core of what I do when I work with my clients. In the process of knowing themselves, they must own and take responsibility for their choices and the actions that have led them to the results they have created.

Follow through.

"Do what you say you are going to do, when you say you are going to do it, in the way you said you were going to do it," says Larry Winget. It is a reminder that follow-through is imperative. If you want to get more of what you want, then you must do what you say and follow through on it.

Act "as if."

You won't always feel as though you can do something, but that should never stop you. When you act "as if," you will find that you will accomplish so much more. And in many cases, as you act "as if," you will grow into that way of being.

Pay attention to the results.

Pay attention to what you accomplish. If a result is not what you want, either put more effort into really doing it or change to an action that will get you what you want. Too often we continue to do what we are doing and then get mad when we keep getting the same results.

"The definition of insanity is doing the same thing over and over and expecting a different result" (Albert Einstein).

Stop settling and tolerating and start setting limits and boundaries.

At the end of my trauma work with a twenty-year-old who had been raped when she was fifteen, we discussed how to evaluate and choose safe people and safe men in her life going forward. We talked about the actions she would need to take in order to ensure that she would not allow herself to tolerate any emotional or physical abuse in her life.

Her background put her at risk for tolerating abusive people in her life, so we discussed ways she could speak up for herself and ask questions that would allow her to determine the character of any future man she would date.

We talked about the quote: "Respect is the minimum." She was determined that, going forward, if she experienced any form of disrespect, she would choose to walk away from the relationship.

This is a perfect example of setting limits and boundaries and then standing up for yourself.

Where are you settling in your life? What limits do you need to set? Decide what you will tolerate and what you will not tolerate. What boundaries do you need to stand up for? Take an action in alignment with those boundaries.

Be Your Best Self

I know that might sound all woo-woo, but we all know when we are being our best self and when we are being our not-so-best self.

When I'm sitting and eating an entire pint of ice cream or avoiding a tough conversation, I know I am not being my best self.

We all have this better part of ourselves. You feel it when we are acting from that place. It is that wise, secure, fully loved part of you. It's the part of you that already has the answer to your problem; it's that part of you that is confident. It's the part that is on the side of LOVE, not fear.

As we grow up, it is easy to lose sight of this part of ourselves. You may even believe you don't have a best self. But you *do* have it. We *all* do!

You, like many people, may have trouble connecting and staying connected to your best self, especially if you are in an emotionally difficult situation. Staying connected to this part of yourself allows you to live from a place where you are more capable to problem solve and manage difficulties more easily. When you are connected to that part of yourself, you live from a place of love and compassion for yourself and others.

When you are connected to your best self, it is possible to live and make choices from your morals and values from a place of integrity.

When you connect to this part of yourself and you are who you want to be, you will get more of what you want.

> **Let's Get Connected to Your Best Self**
>
> Do your own guided imagery in order to connect to your best self. Go somewhere where you won't be disturbed. Sit comfortably and close your eyes. Create a safe, peaceful place in your mind (for example, a beach, a waterfall, a garden). Picture yourself there. Take in the scene around you; notice what you hear, see, and feel. Then, in the distance see a pleasant image coming toward you. This is your best self. Spend time with this part of yourself so you become comfortable with him/her. Ask questions if you like and just listen. When you are ready to leave, tell your best self that you will be coming back.
>
> Practice this several times until you can easily access that part of you. Then you will be able to do this when you are trying to solve a problem or when you're in a difficult situation.

> Happiness is when what you think, what you say, and what you do are in harmony.
>
> —Gandhi

When you stand up for yourself, you will take actions that easily get you more of what you want in your life and relationships.

Now let's put it all together. In the next chapter, I will lay out the plan of how this will look so you can lead a simpler life with better results.

CHAPTER 8

How to Lead a Simpler Life with Better Results

"The unexamined life is not worth living." Socrates supposedly said these words at his trial. They came out of his commitment to his belief that the love of wisdom is the most important pursuit above all else.

Many people live an unintentional life. The biggest problem with living an unintentional life is that you end up creating, without even realizing it, what you do not want.

Everything I have covered in this book so far has been designed to help you learn to live intentionally so you can stop working so hard at getting what you do not want.

> Learn to live intentionally. Learn to live by choice.

Learn to live intentionally. Learn to live by choice. When you don't live by choice, when you don't know yourself, control yourself, speak up, and stand up for yourself, you will continue to get results you don't want.

Living unintentionally can occur in small moments, such as when you yell at your child, criticize your spouse, behave poorly at work, ignore your friend's text, ate that extra piece of pie, or spent money on something you really didn't need. And it can occur in potentially life-altering moments, such as an affair, driving under the influence, having unprotected sex, or yelling at your boss and quitting in a rash moment of anger.

Ultimately, with every unaware choice you make, you are creating the life and results you don't want.

The Unintentional Life

The unintentional life looks like this:

You live from a victim mentality. You live from a place of fear. Living out of your human instinct side, you make choices unconsciously that lead you to be reactive. For a little while you are able to deny or ignore the problems, but eventually judging, criticizing, and blaming creeps in. You defend your right to think, feel, and act the way you do, and you rationalize and resist any other way of looking at it. At some point you just pull away, detaching and withdrawing. Round and round and down and down you go. And the worst of you comes out time and time again. You end up being disconnected from yourself, from the people you love, and from the results you truly desire.

It's a pretty bleak picture, isn't it?

But now you know what you can do to start to live by choice—to turn all of this around.

You are ready to take the steps to live an intentional life and get more of what you want.

Four Steps to Living Intentionally

1) Know yourself.

Know your needs, know the unhelpful beliefs that work against you, know your hot spots, and know your fallback positions. Catch yourself when you are behaving from these places. You know how now. Take action.

I told you I wouldn't leave you stuck in your limited beliefs. Let's replace them with empowered beliefs. You can change your limiting beliefs to empowering beliefs by challenging them, changing them, and then acting as if they are accurate. What you will find is the empowering beliefs eventually do become your truth.

One woman I worked with had this limited belief: "I'm not included." This limited belief made total sense, as she had grown up as the middle child of five siblings and had an alcoholic father. Because of this belief, throughout her adult life she experienced time and time again the feeling of not being included. And when she experienced not being included, she got sad, silent, retreated, and ate a lot. She was left out when it came to her group of friends; in her dating life she tolerated men that often excluded her from their life and activities; and at work she felt not included with a group of co-workers.

After challenging this limited belief, she realized that she did have experiences of being included with her children and siblings, so we changed that belief to "I am included by important people in my life, and I can speak up to make sure others include me." Then she began to speak up. She told her closest friend how she has felt at times and requested to be included and invited even if she was unable to attend. She recognized that the clique she had felt not included in at her job actually had been long-time friends long before they started working at the company, and this allowed her to not be bothered by their friendship. Instead she connected with a few of the newer co-workers. With her husband, she described her childhood wound of not being included, and she asked him to make sure to talk with her about decisions. This changed their relationship, and she felt more connected. By the time we finished our work together, I asked her about the old limited belief. She laughed and said, "Oh, I don't even think about that anymore."

You can change who you are and how you are in the world and in your relationships by knowing yourself and shifting your beliefs and actions.

Let's create an empowering belief:

Write your limited belief from chapter 3:

_____

Ask yourself: "Is that 100 percent accurate? Is it true that I have never, ever in my entire life experienced this limited belief?" For example, "I have never ever felt included in my entire life. No one has ever included me in anything whatsoever." (Go to the extreme sarcastic side.) The answer will be no.

Write three examples where this limited belief was not true:

1) _____

_____

2) _____

_____

3) _____

_____

Then change it to a more helpful empowering belief:

_____

Examples: "I'm incompetent if I ask for help." Change to: "Asking for help is how I learn and grow."

> "I'm not important." Change to: "I'm important to people who care about me."
>
> "I'm not desired." Change to: "I am valued, and I can choose to add more people who value me."
>
> "I'm not respected." Change to: "I am respected, and I don't have to settle."
>
> "I don't feel secure." Change to: "I will choose dependable people I can rely on."
>
> Begin to act as if the empowering belief is true. Choose actions and ways you can speak up and begin living from the empowering belief.

2) Control yourself.

When you train yourself to be aware of your emotions and then control your reactions by taking a time-out and calming yourself, you will at least stop making things messier with your reactions.

Once you've calmed down, you now know how to look at all the negative thoughts and shift your thinking to more positive, helpful thoughts that will work for you.

Positive Psychology research has shown that when it comes to your thoughts, the more grateful and optimistic you are, the happier you will be and the longer you might live. So shifting your thoughts to more positive thoughts and just focusing on the good things you have works to your advantage.

> Gratitude is the healthiest of all human emotions. The more you express gratitude for what you have, the more likely you will have even more to express gratitude for.
>
> —Zig Ziglar

Once you've learned to control your immediate, instinctual feelings and thoughts, you can choose to consistently maneuver through difficulties using more effective ways to handle things so that you can create results that you desire.

Being in control of yourself and managing your thoughts and feelings are more effective ways of handling stressful, difficult situations. The practice of managing your thoughts and feelings is the beginning of being able to shift everything in your life toward more of what you want. Knowing how to manage your thoughts and feelings is a more effective coping mechanism. It's a higher use of *self-observation*. Remember, you can't control something and change it, if you aren't even aware of it.

To help you be even more in control of yourself, instead of automatically using your reactive fallback positions, which gets you nowhere, you can start using more effective, higher defenses from an intentional choice. When I first talked about your fallback positions in chapter 3, I described it as your old, skimpy toolbox. Now that you can utilize self-observation and the following effective coping skills, you have a brand-new fully stocked toolbox. This will help you better manage your difficult feelings, difficult situations, and difficult conflicts so you can stop working so hard and start getting more of what you want.

Here are some additional ways to control yourself:

Humor – Practice seeing the irony in a situation in order to reduce the intensity of it. Become lighthearted and bring laughter into the situation. John Gottman's introduced the idea of the six-second kiss. Whenever things start to get difficult between a couple, one partner blurts out, "Six-second kiss!" The other partner laughs and they'd kiss. It's a great way to maneuver through a conflict and defuse a situation.

Anticipation – Plan ahead when you know you are going into a potentially stressful situation. We all did this every time we studied for a test in school. Do the same thing in other situations. Use the "broken record" technique and plan ahead what you will say. For example, one woman's mother consistently made negative comments about her parenting style. She decided to respond every time her mother said something negative with "Thank you for your suggestion. I will make the best decision for my children."

Suppression – Sometimes the best thing you can do is give yourself some time. I always teach everyone I work with that when they have "big feelings," this is NOT the time to address it. Using suppression is a conscious decision to put off attending to the feelings or thoughts in order to focus on a present situation. This is not denial or avoidance; it is done from a fully conscious place. And you can access the feelings later at a more appropriate time when you have less big emotions about it.

Sublimation – Sublimation and suppression often go together. Sublimation is the ability to divert or shift difficult feelings or thoughts into something socially acceptable. Again, these are not blocked out; they are altered so the focus is on positive actions. For example, you may be upset about a fight at home, but once you get to work, you switch your focus to a special project.

Altruism – This is a conscious decision in which a person temporarily puts their own needs and feelings to the side and becomes of positive service to others. It is managing one's own pain by helping others. For example, after losing your spouse, you decide to volunteer regularly at a soup kitchen.

Affiliation – Affiliation is the idea of turning to other people for support. It's being able to share your problems with another person. However, this is done without the expectation of trying to make the other person responsible for solving them. But if the person just encourages you to stay stuck and ruminate in the negative, that person may not be the best choice.

You now have all that you need to put into practice controlling yourself. If you want to stop working so hard and get more of what you want, controlling your thoughts and feelings and using these additional ways to manage yourself you will get the results you desire.

3) Speak up for yourself.

Speaking up for yourself is considered another one of the higher defenses. You may never have been taught this growing up. But when you get this, it makes all the difference in your relationships and life results.

I worked with an adult daughter and her mother. They had been mad at each other for years and had stopped communicating. I gathered perspectives from both sides. I tried several times to help them to see each other's perspectives, but each of them was locked into believing that they were right. In a final attempt, I printed out a large letter W on a piece of paper. In my next session, as they faced each other, I held the page between the two of them. I ask each woman what letter they saw. The daughter said "W," and her mother said "M." Then I explained, "Yes, it is the same picture, but you each see it differently. That is what is happening when it comes to this disagreement." This finally brought them to an aha moment. They then were able to utilize the tools I taught them to learn more about the each other's perspective. As a result, positive shifts were made in their relationship.

Healthy self-assertion is the ability to hold your own perspective—including your needs, thoughts, and feelings—and be able to communicate to another person in a direct and respectful manner, while at the same time remaining respectful and able to listen to the other's thoughts, feelings, opinions, and needs. Remember the W. It is not about being right and pushing your perspective on others. That will never work for you.

In order to be successful at speaking up for yourself, you must be intentional. Train yourself to approach difficult conversations from the desire to connect with others rather than push against others. Learn to listen deeply and speak up in a way that others will actually want to listen to you.

Mastering these skills will work for you to get more of what you want.

4) Stand up for yourself.

This step is about taking action.

When you take all that you know about yourself, the tools you have learned to control yourself, and the skills to speak up for yourself, now you know what to do. You know right actions to take. You know how to be in the world and how to be in your relationships. When you put all of this into action, you are standing up for yourself. You do this by taking responsibility, doing what you say you are going to do, and following through. You act as if this is who you are even when you don't always feel it, you pay attention to your results, and you change your course of action as needed. You set boundaries and limits and stick to them.

When you take these steps, then you are able to live by choice. You are able to stop working so hard doing what you shouldn't do.

You now live by choice.

Living by Choice (The Intentional Life)

The intentional life looks like this:

When you take the steps to live by choice, life is much more enjoyable and you will, with more ease, get more of what you want.

I'd love to say that you'll never go back to the human instinct side, but that's not how it works. However, what does change is how long you stay on the miserable side and how quickly you can get out of that side—because now you have all the tools to move yourself back to the intentional side.

When you live an intentional life, you live from an empowered place, an expansive place based on love.

You are able to be proactive, take responsibility for yourself, take conscious, wise actions, and have more acceptance, empathy, and compassion for yourself and for those around you. You are able to forgive others, repair relationships, and learn and grow. You spiral upward, becoming your best self and creating a deeper connection to yourself and to those that matter most in your life.

> Your thoughts, your words, and your actions created the life you are living.
> You create your results—no one else.
> —Larry Winget

As Larry Winget says, "Your thoughts, your words, and your actions created the life you are living. You create your results—no one else."

When you live an intentional life, you become the best version of yourself. You are able to stop working so hard and not getting what you want. Instead you get the results, the relationships, and the life you really want.

Begin to LIVE BY CHOICE!

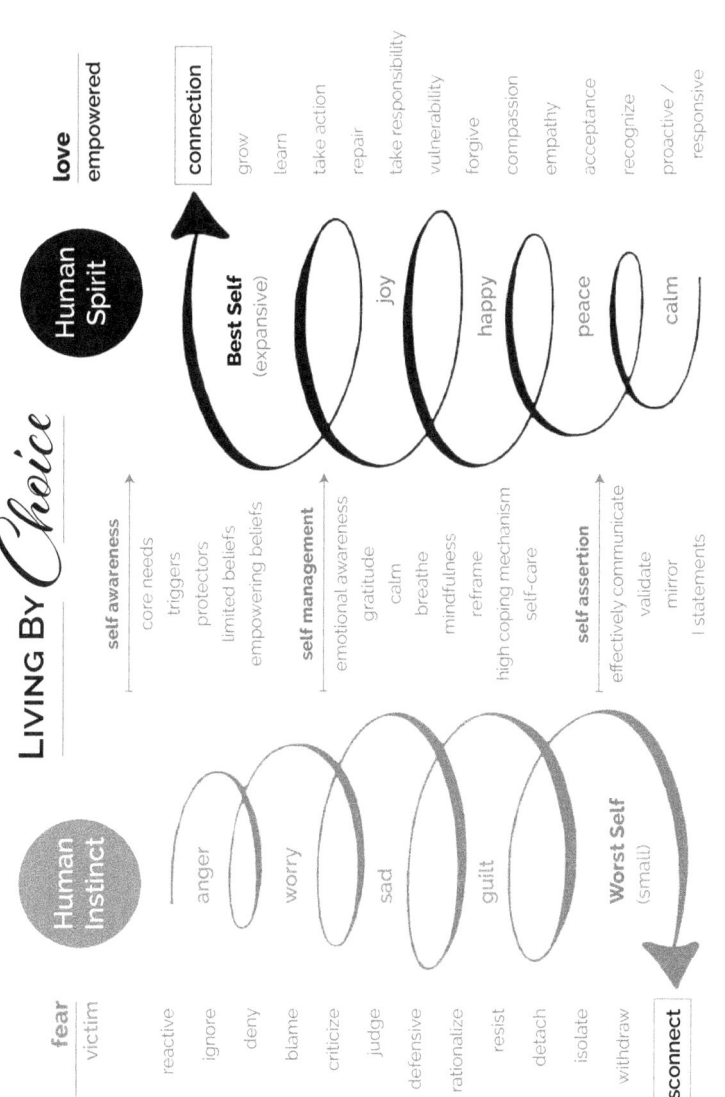

CHAPTER 9

Getting More of What You Do Want

Now you know the ways you have been working way too hard and still not getting what you want.

I know you have been doing a *million* things to try to make it right, and you're exhausted. You are blaming yourself. You are blaming everyone else. You are going in the wrong direction and consistently getting the opposite of what you want. When really all you ever had to do was figure out who you are and why you are that way and then get control of the way you think, act, and react. Then you are better prepared to go into each situation and speak up and stand up in a way that moves you to resolution and creates the results you want.

That's as hard as anything has to be. That's as hard as it has to be when dealing with clients, with your boss or co-workers, with your kids, or with your spouse. That's as hard as it has to be when you are dealing with anyone in any relationship of any kind, and even with your relationship with money, with food, and with your body. You've got to go through these steps.

> As human beings, our greatness lies not so much in being able to remake the world as in being able to remake ourselves.
>
> —Gandhi

Gandhi says, "As human beings, our greatness lies not so much in being able to remake the world as in being able to remake ourselves." It's time to remake yourself. It doesn't have to be so difficult. You've got the steps now. You know what you need to do.

You need to ask yourself some questions and then take action.

- Do I really know who I am and why I am that way?
- Am I able to control my feelings and negative thoughts?
- Am I able to control myself?
- Will my words and will my actions move me to resolution so I get more of what I want?

The faster you are able to do this, the more success, happiness, and connection you will have.

When you practice these steps and get good at them, they become who you are. So you see, who you are doesn't have to be who you've always been. Who you are is the person you've created based on using these tools.

Now, to quickly help get you going in the right direction, based on everything you have gathered from this book, choose one action you will start doing in the following areas of your life. Set a date and start doing it. Remember, nothing will change without action.

What's one step you can take to improve your money situation? (pay off your highest interest rate credit card first, pay an extra twenty dollars per month on your credit card, go through your house and find five things you don't need and sell it on the internet, create a monthly automatic transfer to your savings account, track your spending)

Write down one step you will implement:

_____

Start Date: _____

What's one step you can take to improve your weight/health situation? (go to the doctor so you know what your important health numbers are, eat on a smaller plate, create a cut off time you will stop eating at night, walk twenty minutes every day, hire a personal trainer)

Write down one step you will implement:

_____

Start Date: _____

What's one step you can take to improve your significant other relationship? (take five minutes a day to tell them what you appreciate about them, say thank you, buy a small gift for them, stop and share three fond memories with them)

Write down one step you will implement:

_____

Start Date: _____

What's one step you can take to improve your relationships with your kids? (spend thirty minutes of one-on-one time a week with your child, make a point to find five things a day they do well and praise them, apologize when you are wrong)

Write down one step you will implement:

_____

Start Date: _____

What's one step you can take to improve a family member relationship? (send a card letting them know what's something they did that was helpful for you growing up, go on a lunch date with them, ask them what's going on in their life)

Write down one step you will implement:

_____

Start Date: _____

What's one step you can take to improve a friendship?
(send a card letting them know what you appreciate about them, go out to lunch or coffee with them, ask them what's going on in their life)

Write down one step you will implement:

_____

Start Date: _____

> What's one step you can take to improve your job situation?
> (ask your boss for feedback on one area you can improve in, think about the job you were hired to do and at the end of each day evaluate if you did it, look for other jobs out there that might better utilize your skills)
>
> Write down one step you will implement:
>
> _____
>
> Start Date: _____

> What's one step you can take to improve your business (if you run your own business)?
> (schedule a daily time for follow-up calls, ask people to hire you, take a sales training, hire a business coach, schedule a weekly time to develop your business)
>
> Write down one step you will implement:
>
> _____
>
> Start Date: _____

> Yesterday I was clever, so I wanted to change the world.
> Today I am wise, so I am changing myself.
> —Rumi

Rumi said, "Yesterday I was clever, so I wanted to change the world. Today I am wise, so I am changing myself." To change your world, you need to start by changing yourself. Stop working so hard at getting what you don't want.

You know the steps.

Know who you are and why you are that way. Who you are and why you are that way makes you think, act, and react in certain ways.

Then **get control** of how you think, act, and react. When you get control of how you think, act, and react, you no longer have to be who you've been. Instead you can begin creating who you want to be—able to **speak up for yourself** and **stand up for yourself** so you can take the right action and finally get what you want in your life and relationships.

> **Know who you** are and why you are that way. Who you are and why you are that way makes you think, act, and react in certain ways.
>
> Then **get control** of how you think, act, and react. When you get control of how you think, act, and react, you no longer have to be who you've been. Instead you can begin creating who you want to be—able to **speak up for yourself** and **stand up for yourself** so you can take the right action and finally get what you want in your life and relationships.

This is your new plan. I work with people all the time and take them through these exact same steps. At the end of our work they consistently tell me:

- "I wish I had known this before."
- "I'm so much happier."
- "Life is so much better now."

You can have these results too!

If you want to stop working so hard and getting results you don't really want, you are going to have to, at some point, go through this process. You can't escape it unless you want to keep beating your head against the wall, working too hard, being exhausted, being depressed, blaming yourself, blaming others, and still not getting the results you want. If you go through all these steps, you will start leading a simpler life with better results—and isn't that why we all wake up every morning and go through our day? We hope and believe we will have more of what we want in our life and in our relationships.

Changing your world and your relationships starts with changing yourself.

> Changing your world and your relationships starts with changing yourself.

You've got this! Now go do it!

www.ingramcontent.com/pod-product-compliance
Lightning Source LLC
Chambersburg PA
CBHW071420070526
44578CB00003B/624